HOOVER VS
THE SECO

CW00971600

AN OPERATION PRIME TIME EVENT

A SALTZMAN/GLICKMAN/SELZNICK
PRESENTATION

A SUNRISE FILMS LIMITED PRODUCTION

STARRING

JACK WARDEN as J. Edgar Hoover
NICHOLAS CAMPBELL as Robert Kennedy
ROBERT PINE as John F. Kennedy
BARRY MORSE as Joseph Kennedy Sr.

Introducing
LELAND GANTT as Martin Luther King
Special Appearance
by HEATHER THOMAS as Marilyn Monroe
and RICHARD ANDERSON as Lyndon Johnson

Produced by Paul Saltzman
Directed by Michael O'Herlihy
Executive Producers Daniel Selznick and Joel
Glickman
Written by Lionel E. Siegel

To Kitty

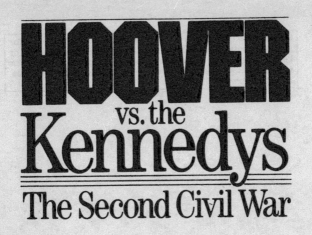

HOOVER
vs. the
Kennedys
The Second Civil War

Christopher Cook Gilmore

ST. MARTIN'S PRESS/NEW YORK

HOOVER VS. THE KENNEDY'S: THE SECOND CIVIL WAR

ISBN: 0-312-90997-7   Can. ISBN: 0-312-90998-5

Printed in the United States of America

First St. Martin's Press mass market edition/November 1987

10 9 8 7 6 5 4 3 2 1

Prologue

John Edgar Hoover glared at the television set, grunted, and put another grape in his mouth. On screen the delegates to the 1960 Democratic Convention were clapping their hands, stamping their feet, and chanting, "Kennedy, Kennedy, Kennedy!" Disgusted, Hoover spat out a grape pit and looked toward the bedroom.

"Junior?"

Clyde Tolson entered the room carrying some thin files. He stood beside his boss, waiting. Tolson had once been a strikingly handsome man, but now, at sixty, those looks were fading quickly. Hoover, flaccid and portly, was sixty-five, and had been director of the FBI since 1924. He patted the couch next to him and nodded toward the TV. Obediently, Tolson sat down and watched. In the Los Angeles Sports Arena, Richard Daley, mayor of Chicago, stood up and announced that his state, the glorious state of Illinois, was casting fifty-nine-and-a-half votes for Senator Kennedy . . . and two votes for Illinois Governor Adlai Stevenson. As the delegates erupted in a new outburst, Hoover turned down the sound.

"That surprise you, Junior? Let me tell you something. If you had Daley and that mobster Giancana and his goons strongarming the wards like Kennedy probably did, *you* could have taken Illinois."

Tolson lowered his eyes.

"Well, that's the end of Adlai. We're finally rid of that egghead fruitcake and his pinko pal, Eleanor Roosevelt. What have you got for me?" Hoover held out his hand.

Tolson gave him the first of the files. "I thought this might interest you, Edgar. It's the latest on that congressman and his chief fundraiser. Hot stuff."

Hoover scanned a series of eight-by-ten glossy photographs. He smiled and licked his lips, then put them aside. "What else?"

Tolson handed over the rest of the files. "John Kennedy's still having his assignations with Marilyn Monroe."

"At his own sister and brother-in-law's house. Disgusting."

Tolson nodded. "The Nixon surveillance hasn't been very productive, I'm afraid."

"Of course not. Nixon's a man of solid moral values, Junior. What did you expect?"

Tolson stood up. "Is there anything else you'd like, Edgar?"

Hoover's mood shifted quickly. Scowling at his subordinate, he snarled, "I'd like to know what's going on around here."

Tolson blanched. "Sir?"

"Look at those fruitbaskets!"

Tolson regarded the twin fruitbaskets, gifts of the Del Charro Hotel management, resting side by side on the coffee table. Nothing seemed amiss. He looked back at his boss and waited.

"Don't give me that innocent look, Clyde. You must have an in with the bell captain, huh? You got one more peach than I did!"

Tolson sprang to the coffee table and switched the baskets. "Edgar, I swear, I didn't even look. They must have given me yours, really."

"I'll bet."

Tolson picked up a wrapped package. "Why, you haven't opened this yet."

Hoover took the package with a look of disgust. "What for? It's the same damn bottle of booze . . . the same for how many years? Fifteen, twenty?"

"You never know, Edgar. They may have changed brands this year."

"You're worse than a kid." Hoover opened the package, a bottle of twelve-year-old scotch. He put it on the coffee table. "Our annual gift from the mayor of La Jolla, California. Considering

3

how many years we've been coming here, the least they could do is give us a hot tip for Del Mar . . . and a couple of $500 bills."

Hoover's black mood was over. Tolson relaxed, went to the fireplace, and lit the gas log. "I've already got my bets figured out for tomorrow."

"I'll do my own handicapping, thank you. Hand me that racing form."

Tolson did as he was told.

Part I

CHAPTER 1

"I can almost taste this moment." Joseph Kennedy Sr. nodded toward his son, but could not tear his eyes from the television screen. The crucial moment of the delegate balloting was imminent; the Democratic National Convention was about to throw its full endorsement to JFK.

"It's not over until it's over," said John Fitzgerald Kennedy. The youthful senator from Massachusetts helped himself to more lobster. The two men were alone in the breakfast room of their friend Marion Davies' Los Angeles estate, a sprawling mansion on a par with the Kennedy homes back East. This was the moment the father and son had been waiting for all these weeks.

On the TV screen the chairman of the Wyoming delegation rose to his feet, and for a few seconds the entire Los Angeles Sports Arena was hushed. John Kennedy lowered his fork and looked at his hands. They were cool and steady.

". . . that the proud state of Wyoming casts its fifteen votes . . . for the next president of the United States . . . John Fitzgerald Kennedy!"

Joseph Kennedy embraced his son. There were tears in the old man's eyes and a lump in his throat. John Kennedy could feel his father's heart beat against him.

On screen a newscaster blurted, ". . . seven hundred and sixty-one votes! He's won the Democratic presidential nomination on the first vote!"

John Kennedy patted his father's back. "I couldn't have done it without you, Dad."

"It's your brother Bobby you have to thank, son. He's the organizer. All I did was write some checks and phone a few old friends."

"I shall always be grateful for everything you've done."

"It's my dream come true, son. And you've done it!"

John Kennedy smiled, sat down, and cracked a lobster claw. "I haven't done it yet, Dad. There's still Nixon between me and the White House."

The elder Kennedy, trembling and glassy-eyed, bent over and squinted at the screen. "Don't worry about Nixon, John. We'll beat Nixon. We'll beat 'em all!"

* * *

Late that night, hours after JFK had officially accepted the presidential nomination, Bobby Kennedy, who served as his campaign manager, was huddled with Byron "Whizzer" White, a member of the Kennedy campaign team, in an eighth-floor suite of the Los Angeles Biltmore Hotel. Both men were agitated.

"Bobby, without Lyndon Johnson on the ticket, Jack won't carry a single southern state. With LBJ you get Texas, and because he's Protestant you get a good shot at some other electoral votes."

Bobby held up both hands. "I know. But if Lyndon accepts the vice-presidential spot we lose our labor support."

"Maybe."

"At any rate," said Bobby with a shrug, "I can't believe Lyndon will take the number-two slot. His ego won't let him."

At that moment, flashing his winning smile, John Kennedy entered the room. "I've got a big surprise for you, Bobby," he said. "Lyndon's accepted."

Bobby groaned. "You're not serious!"

Jack nodded, accepting a drink from Whizzer White.

Bobby was furious. "LBJ's a crude old cornball. He could lose the North for us. Jack, most of the people who support us hate him!"

Jack sipped his highball. "I just had the same argument with Dad. It gets down to this: I have

9

no choice. If I want to be elected I've got to have Lyndon along."

"What if we offered him something else?" asked White.

"Like what?"

"Let me talk to him," said Bobby. "Maybe I can talk him into taking another job."

Rubbing his temples, Jack thought a moment, then looked at his brother. "Okay. Give it a try. But remember, Bobby, we don't want to make him an enemy."

Bobby left the room. A few minutes later he was in Johnson's suite on the fifth floor, alone with the man he despised. Johnson sat and listened, watching Bobby like a hawk.

". . . it's ugly, Lyndon. It's deadly. They've told me flat out that if we announce you for vice-presidential candidate they'll stage a floor fight to challenge you. They'll blow this convention wide open! They'll not only damage us, but they'll destroy you, Lyndon."

Johnson lowered his head and said nothing.

"There's only one other powerful position that would be worthy of your talents. In significant ways it's much more visible and influential than the vice presidency would be. You could be chairman of the national Democratic party, Lyndon."

Johnson remained silent.

"Talk about a power base, Lyndon! There is nothing that could match it except the presidency. After Senator Kennedy's been in for two terms you'd be . . ."

Bobby's voice trailed off as Johnson raised his head and looked at him, tears streaming down his face. Johnson's voice faltered as he spoke. "I want to be the vice president, Bobby. I don't want to be anything else. Jack promised me. It's . . . the only job I want."

Bobby Kennedy was defeated and he knew it.

CHAPTER 2

The following morning when John F. Kennedy stepped in the shower and adjusted the water temperature, Marilyn Monroe let out a scream.

"Too cold!"

John made another adjustment.

"Too hot!"

He made a very fine and careful adjustment to both knobs.

"That's better, Mr. President."

At thirty-one Marilyn had kept her youthful figure and smooth skin. JFK noted this as he lathered her down. "I'm not the president yet, Marilyn. I was only nominated last night."

Marilyn rinsed herself, took the soap, and lathered Jack. "Wow," she exclaimed, reacting to the surgical scars on his back. "Your poor back . . ."

Jack laughed. "You should have seen the other guy."

Marilyn traced the scars with her fingertips. "Seriously, Jack, is it true you almost died twice?"

Jack slapped her bottom playfully and demanded, "Is this a romantic interlude or are you doing an article for *Cosmopolitan?*"

She moved around in front of him, flashing her famous smile. "It's just something I heard . . ."

"It's true. They administered last rites to me twice." He winked at her. "They say the third time's the lucky one."

She kissed him. "I don't feel sorry for you, if that's what you're thinking."

"Good."

"I just want to understand you, that's all."

Jack put his hands on her shoulders and smiled. "I'm easy, Marilyn. I just live one day at a time." He dropped the soap, bent down, and pretended to have difficulty finding it. Marilyn squealed, pulled him up, and hugged him. "But what about tomorrow, Jack? What about . . ."

He interrupted her gently. "No. Nothing else. Yesterday's dead, tomorrow's unborn. Today is all that's real. It's all there is."

She slipped from his arms, stepped out of the shower, and grabbed a big, white bath towel. "Time to dry off . . . Mr. President nominee . . ."

* * *

The first day of the Southern Christian Leadership Conference in Atlanta, Georgia, was a gray one. Clouds wafted by overhead, and the air smelled like rain. The old and battered SCLC building had its doors open wide as a well-worn blue Chevrolet pulled up to the curb and stopped. From it stepped the Reverend Martin Luther King, Jr., the Reverend Ralph Abernathy, and two of their advisors. On the sidewalk two young black men approached. They shook hands with King, who introduced them to Abernathy.

"Ernest Royce and Lamar Evans. These young men are organizing a sit-in at the local lunch counters."

"Now?" asked Abernathy.

"What's wrong with now, Reverend?" asked Lamar.

King spoke up. "The sit-ins are a fine idea. But I'm not sure the timing's right. It might be a mistake to do anything before the presidential election in November."

Ernest frowned. "What you mean is you've already promised your Kennedy and Nixon friends that us colored folks wouldn't make any trouble until after the white folks have had their elections, right?"

It was King's turn to frown. "We have made no such agreement."

Lamar spoke up. "The elections have about as much to do with us as the Kentucky Derby, Reverend King. We came here to ask you to join us in the sit-ins. October the nineteenth is when we're gonna do it. Seven stores in downtown Atlanta."

Ernest was pleading. "Can we tell everybody you're with us, Reverend?"

"I don't know," said King. "Of course I'm with you, but I may not be able to come to Atlanta on the nineteenth. That's the day I'm scheduled to meet Jack Kennedy in Miami. I'll have to let you know."

The two young men exchanged a look.

"Thanks for taking the time, y'all," said Ernest. They turned abruptly and walked away.

Abernathy was offended. "Audacious, rude, stubborn, insulting, defiant, and downright insolent. I leave anything out, Martin?"

King smiled sadly. "You left out . . . Thank God for them. Thank God for those young men . . ."

On the evening of October 18, 1960, J. Edgar Hoover approached the podium of the national convention of the American Legion, waited several minutes for the applause to die, then cleared his throat and spoke his mind.

". . . The diabolical influence of communism on youth was manifested in the Communist-inspired riots in San Francisco this year against a congressional committee. These students were stooges of a sinister technique stimulated by clever Communist propagandists who remained quietly in the background . . ."

Hoover was interrupted by shouts of encouragement, which he acknowledged with a friendly wave, then continued.

"Alarming, too, is the ease with which some major educational institutions have been duped under the much-abused term of 'academic freedom.' Our nation is coming under attack from a new breed I call 'pseudo-liberal internationalists' for whom patriotism has become a dirty word, belief in God old-fashioned, if not ridiculous . . ."

He was drowned out by a standing ovation.

Coretta King, six months pregnant, hugged little Martin III to her and tried to control her tears. With shaking hands she dialed a number in Washington, D.C., the JFK election headquarters, and asked to speak to Harris Wofford, the campaign's civil rights coordinator. When he got on the phone she blurted, "They're going to kill him, Harris! I know it!"

"What's wrong, Coretta?"

"Martin was arrested at the sit-ins in Atlanta."

"Coretta, there's nothing to worry about. Martin's been arrested how many times? They'll release him and . . ."

"No! They've released all the demonstrators except Martin! They kept him in the jail! Supposedly it's because he was on probation for driving in Georgia with his Alabama driver's license."

"As soon as they set bail he'll be free, Coretta."

"He's been refused bail, Harris. They've sentenced him to *four months at hard labor!*"

"Why, that's crazy . . ."

"They're sending Martin to a chain gang! Harris, you're close to Senator Kennedy. He must be able to do something. I've called everybody else we know, and they all say they don't know what to do. They say they can't fight a judge."

"What's the judge's name, Coretta?"

"Judge Mitchell, DeKalb County. You'll talk to Senator Kennedy, won't you, Harris?"

"Immediately."

That same evening Coretta King appeared on television, talking to a reporter. "I have spoken with Senator Kennedy. He was most kind and offered to give me any assistance I might need . . ."

J. Edgar Hoover, at his home in Washington, D.C., was watching the show. Nearby, Special Agent James Crawford, a middle-aged black man employed by Hoover as a butler, was polishing silver trays and objects, while Annie Fields, the housekeeper, served tea.

"What do you think of that, Junior?" Clyde Tolson sat on the floor, holding Hoover's pet terrier, G-boy.

"They say King is a clever man, Edgar. But he sure wasn't too smart letting himself get locked up in Georgia."

Hoover laughed. "Well, brains ain't the coloreds' strongest suit."

Hoover's butler and housekeeper paused, then went on with their chores.

"I guess not, Edgar," said Tolson, playing with the dog.

"You know their brains are twenty percent smaller than ours?" Hoover wasn't joking.

"That so?"

Crawford and Fields looked at each other and cringed. A moment later they were back at work. Hoover's comments were, after all, nothing new. They came with the job.

CHAPTER 3

Bobby Kennedy was furious. He looked around the room for a target. John Seigenthaler, Byron White, Nicholas Katzenbach, Louis Martin, and Harris Wofford stared back at him. Wofford couldn't hide his guilt. Bobby saw it, but let it go.

"Okay. I don't give a damn who talked Jack into calling Mrs. King. But understand this: no one is to make any comment of any kind about that call. A couple of senators from the South just told me in no uncertain terms that they're worried that Jack might support Martin Luther King. If he does, they're ready to give their support to Nixon. Remember, the election is just around the corner."

Bobby sat down at his desk and picked up a file, a signal to his aides that he wanted to be alone.

Dutifully they rose and filed out, all except Harris Wofford, who closed the door, leaned against it, and faced Kennedy. Bobby put down the file.

"Okay, Harris, spill it."

"How would you like to spend four months on a Georgia chain gang . . . because you're black?" Wofford placed a slip of paper on Bobby's desk. He left without another word.

That evening after dinner Ethel Kennedy sat with her husband before a crackling fire in the hearth of their home, Hickory Hill. Bobby was preoccupied, and had been all through dinner.

"What's the matter, Bobby?"

Kennedy sighed. "The world is full of contradictions."

"This we know." She handed him a cocktail.

"What I mean is . . . *I'm* full of contradictions."

"Drink."

Bobby sipped his drink and put it down. He hugged his wife. "Ethel, today I stormed around the office warning everyone not to comment on Jack's call to Mrs. King because of what it would cost us in southern votes. And tonight . . . right now . . . I'm thinking of what a mockery of justice it is to put that man in jail, to put him on a chain gang for four months for a traffic violation. God, if only there was something I could do."

"Do what you think is right."

"Sure, but what's right? The election is in eleven days. Those southern Democrats are just waiting for an excuse to dump us. If I help King . . ."

"Bobby, if you do what is right you'll never fail, you'll never lose at anything."

"What am I supposed to do? Phone the judge? I'm a lawyer. Lawyers aren't allowed to influence judges. I could be disbarred."

"Do you know who the judge is?"

Bobby took a crumpled slip of paper from his pocket and looked at it miserably. "Judge Mitchell. Harris Wofford gave me his phone number."

Ethel handed him the phone. Bobby kissed her. Then he smiled, shrugged, and dialed.

"Judge Mitchell? Judge Mitchell, this is Bobby Kennedy. I'm sorry to be calling at this hour. Well, sir, I'll tell you what's on my mind. You and I are fellow Democrats, and we've got a problem. We need your help.

"You see, sir, we've got a real tough election in just a few days, and we don't want the Republicans to win. That's just not what the country needs, it's not what any of us needs. Yes, sir, that's right.

"Well, sir, it's about Dr. King. If you keep him in jail without bail we Democrats are going to look awful foolish. We will be leaving Mr. Nixon a wide-open chance to ridicule us. If you keep King in jail we don't gain a single vote, but we stand to lose a lot. But if you let him out on bail

23

you show the country that southern justice is fair. We win a lot of votes and help assure a Democratic party victory.

"Yes, sir. Please, just think about it, yes. And thank you for taking my call, Judge Mitchell. Good-bye."

By nine o'clock the following morning, Martin Luther King, Jr., was a free man.

That afternoon the operator of an elevator on the first floor of the Justice Department Building in Washington, D.C. held open the doors of his car a few seconds longer than usual. An impatient man in a brown three-piece suit stared at the operator and snapped, "Let's go."

"Just a moment, sir." The operator peered down the hallway and kept his hand on the control. A second later Clyde Tolson and another FBI agent appeared, followed closely by J. Edgar Hoover. They entered the elevator and instantly the doors closed and the elevator rose.

"Third floor," ordered the impatient man.

The operator nodded, but the car kept going, stopping at the fifth floor. Hoover and his agents stepped into the corridor.

"I'm going to complain about this!" said the brown-suited man. The doors slid shut in his face.

Hoover and his agents strode briskly down the corridor. Their path was blocked momentarily by a twenty-year-old mail clerk pushing a heavily laden mail cart. The boy was good-looking, had a slight case of acne, and was wearing a gray suit with a bright red corduroy vest. When he had gone, Hoover nodded in his direction and spoke quietly to Tolson. "We're not going to have anyone working for us who has a pimply face and wears a red vest. Get rid of him."

"Yessir."

"And fire whoever hired him."

At his desk in his inner office, Hoover pushed a button, and the television came on. On screen a reporter was interviewing Martin Luther King, his father, his wife Coretta, and Ralph Abernathy. Hoover grunted, then shouted into the intercom, "Junior? Get in here!"

"How was life on the chain gang, Reverend King?" asked the reporter.

Martin Luther King smiled widely at the camera. "Well, I didn't get to taste it, thank God. Judge Mitchell decided to release me on bail."

Hoover shot Tolson a disgusted look.

King continued. "I'm a free man thanks to my wife's efforts. And I am deeply indebted to Senator Kennedy, who served as a great force in securing my release."

Abernathy broke in. "What Reverend King means is that it's time to take off our Nixon buttons."

"Do you agree with your son, Reverend King?"

"Absolutely," replied King, Sr. "I had expected to vote against Senator Kennedy because of his religion. But now he can be my president, Catholic or whatever he is . . ."

On signal from his boss, Tolson changed the channel.

Less than a mile away, in the JFK campaign headquarters, Bobby Kennedy, Seigenthaler, Wofford, and the highest-ranking black member of the campaign staff, Louis Martin, were watching the same show. The men were elated; Martin Luther King may win some votes, after all.

"Senator Kennedy has the moral courage to stand up for what he knows is right," said King, looking directly into the camera.

Coretta King, visibly pregnant, added, "I called a lot of people to try and get help for my husband. Senator Kennedy responded, Mr. Nixon remained silent. I am going to return his silence when I go to the voting booth."

When the newscast was over Wofford nudged Bobby. "You called the judge?"

Bobby nodded.

Seigenthaler spoke up. "You checked with Jack first, right?"

Bobby shook his head. Louis Martin laughed.

"What's so funny, Mr. Martin?" Bobby asked.

"It does my heart good," said Martin, "to know you white folks in high places are just as confused and disorganized as we colored folks."

Bobby grinned. "Well, we either won it by

gaining the Negro vote, or blew it by losing the South."

"Let's not kid ourselves," said Martin. "The Negro voters have to know about this first. They can't be reached by TV. The Negro newspapers are weeklies, so we've missed their deadlines. We'll have to do something to get the story out."

"I'll take care of it," said Harris Wofford.

Clyde Tolson wanted to see his boss, but had to wait. Hoover's receptionist, sixty-year-old Miss Helen Gandy, stopped him at the door. "He won't be long, Clyde," she said, looking at her watch. "He's entertaining some Girl Scouts from Youngstown, Ohio."

Suddenly a red light on Miss Gandy's desk began flashing. Sam Noisette, fifty-six, Hoover's personal servant—although he was carried on the books as an FBI agent—stood up and looked at his watch. "I hope Jack doesn't screw up again."

"Jack's gone," said Miss Gandy. "We got a younger man." At that moment a young man rushed into the office holding a large camera. Miss Gandy opened the door to Hoover's office and the young man sprang inside.

"Yep," said Miss Gandy, looking at her watch again, "he's already broken Jack's best time."

Tolson followed Noisette through the door and waited while J. Edgar Hoover posed for pictures with the awed Girl Scouts and their den mother. The photographer took three pictures and rushed out. Hoover smiled at the girls. "Now Mr. Noisette will take you on the special tour we've arranged. When you get back I'll give you each a copy of the picture we just took and autograph it."

"Right this way, ladies," said Sam, ushering them out.

Tolson waited for the FBI director to seat himself behind his desk, then handed him a pamphlet, a play-by-play description of Martin Luther King's release from prison.

"Kennedy's campaign people had almost two million of these printed and circulated to every Negro church in the country last Sunday," said Tolson.

Hoover looked bored. "Don't worry, Junior. The colored don't come out to vote much. It's too complicated for them. Nixon will be elected and that's certain." He threw the pamphlet in the wastebasket. "Next."

Tolson handed him a letter from the top of a large stack. Hoover read the first paragraph, turned red, and slammed his fist on the desk.

"I told you it was going to happen again, and it did!"

"Sir?"

"For the second year in a row the Masonic lodge has refused to allow me to become a thirty-third degree Mason! Me!" He scowled at Tolson. "I *told* you to take care of it! Now don't tell me I didn't, I know I did! What do I have to do, Clyde? Go down there myself and conduct an investigation?"

The obsequious Tolson straightened his tie, hurrying to reply, "No, Edgar. I'll . . ."

"It's somebody in the Arlington lodge that's blackballed me! I'm positive of that. Probably that old pal of Truman's!"

"I'll give it my immediate attention, Edgar." Tolson hurried out.

Alone, Hoover sat scowling for a few minutes. Taking a key from his pocket, he unlocked his lower desk drawer and took out a file. In it was a thick pile of photos, black-and-white pictures of a nude man and woman in bed. Shaking his head disapprovingly, he pushed a button and spoke into the intercom.

"Miss Gandy? See that I'm not disturbed for the next half hour."

It was too late, he was told. The Girl Scouts were back from their tour. Hoover put away the pictures and put on his best smile.

Three days later, at 8:30 A.M., Bobby Kennedy who hadn't yet been to sleep, led his wife up the stairs to the second floor of John Fitzgerald Kennedy's spacious Hyannisport house, and knocked on Jack and Jackie's bedroom door. There was no answer. Ethel knocked again.

"Come back later." It was JFK's sleepy voice.

Ethel spoke. "It's sort of . . . important, Jack."

They heard a yawn, then, "Okay, Ethel. Come on in."

Bobby and Ethel burst in, both of them grinning from ear to ear. "Congratulations . . . Mr. President!"

Jack opened his arms and shouted for joy. Jackie and Ethel hugged him, shouting, laughing, crying. After a moment they grew quiet and let him go. Jack stood and looked at himself in the mirror. He was different now; he knew it—they all knew it.

Everything was different now.

CHAPTER 4

The next two weeks passed quickly. JFK, the new president of the United States, was back from Washington, D.C. for a weekend of relaxation at Hyannisport. At noon on Sunday, his father suggested they take a walk in the garden. When they were alone, Joe Kennedy brought up the subject of presidential appointments.

"Well, Dad, everyone whose opinion I respect urges me to get rid of Hoover and Dulles. They're treacherous."

Joe Kennedy paused before his rose bushes. He shook his head and spoke carefully. "Jack, you won the election by a hair. The right-wing Republicans in Congress think Dulles is necessary to protect the country. They think Hoover is necessary to keep the Communists from taking over."

John Kennedy nodded, listening carefully.

"Son, your opponents in Congress expect you to dump Hoover and Dulles. In fact, they're itching for you to do just that. But you're too smart to pull a dumb stunt like that. You'll just make enemies. You'll cripple yourself. Now here's my advice. You reappoint both of them. Do it before you appoint anyone else. *Then,* maybe you can get something passed through Congress."

Jack smiled, narrowed his eyes. "I don't suppose keeping Hoover on has anything to do with the fact that he's an old friend of yours."

"Of course not!" his father snapped. "Wise up, Jack. You've got lots of ideas to help the country, lots of laws you want to get passed. Don't turn Congress against you before you've gotten started."

"How about a compromise? What if I fire just one of them?"

The elder Kennedy frowned. "Be serious. After Dulles and Hoover you appoint Bobby. Make him attorney general. You've got to have someone around you who will always tell you the truth."

JFK had a twinkle in his eye. "What about Jackie and Ethel? You figure they should be in the cabinet?"

Joe winced. "I love your sense of humour, Jack . . . in its place. You may laugh, but I'm telling you you'll need Bobby by your side from day one. You can wait on Teddy . . ."

"Dad, if I make Bobby attorney general I'll be attacked by every newspaper in the country. He's got no experience for the job. Besides, I just promised the job to Ribicoff."

Joe Kennedy turned on his heel and resumed the garden stroll. Jack smiled at the old man, shook his head, and followed.

". . . Senator McClellan said that if I took the attorney general's job it would hurt Jack. What do you think?" In J. Edgar Hoover's office, Bobby Kennedy was posing the question to the man himself. Hoover sat at his desk, watching the younger man pace the floor.

"It could be," he said.

"How badly, Edgar?" Bobby leaned on his desk.

"Hard to say."

"Would you take the job?"

Hoover looked up. "You mean today? Now?"

"Sure."

"Maybe. Yes, maybe I would . . ."

"Attorney General Rogers said it was a lousy job."

"That a fact?"

Bobby Kennedy was pushing the FBI director. He pushed harder.

"Now that you've been reappointed, Edgar, I thought I ought to get your opinion. After all, if I took the appointment we'd be working together."

Hoover smiled, put his hands behind his head,

and leaned back. "You know, I just got a picture in my mind of you and your father, right here in this office. But you were seven or eight years old then, and your socks were always falling down."

Bobby chuckled. "Yes, I think you gave me a card or something. It said FBI on it. I showed it to all my friends."

"How proud and pleased your dear mother must be of both you boys. Teddy, too, of course."

"She is indeed."

Hoover looked out the window for a moment, then turned to Bobby. "Robert," he said after a pause, "I'm not the best person to ask about the attorney general's job, because even though in theory he's my superior, I always deal *directly* with the president."

"Yes?"

"However, I have every confidence in your abilities. Despite what others have told you, I think you'd make a fine attorney general."

"You do?"

"Most certainly. And don't feel defensive because your brother is president. The Dulles brothers have set an enviable record in government." Hoover stood, moved around his desk to Bobby, and shook his hand.

"Thanks, Edgar," Bobby said. "I value your opinion. Good-bye."

"My best wishes to your father," Hoover added as Bobby walked out the door. A moment later Clyde Tolson entered by another door.

Hoover looked at him and shrugged. "What else could I tell him?"

Tolson nodded. "You know, Edgar, you're really to blame for where Jack Kennedy has gotten to."

Hoover knew what he meant, but pretended he did not.

"Why, what do you mean, Junior?"

"You've forgotten? Back during the war, Edgar. You found out that Lieutenant Commander John F. Kennedy was keeping company with that Scandinavian lady who had Nazi friends. You passed on the word and the next day Kennedy was transferred to combat aboard a PT boat in the Pacific."

"Oh, that . . ."

Tolson held up a finger. "So it's your fault that Kennedy became a hero, wrote a best-selling book about his war experiences, and got elected president."

Hoover laughed, then grew serious. "Junior, I'm not at all worried about Jack Kennedy."

"You're not?"

"Don't you see? Jack is Joe's boy. Joe Kennedy and I go back a long way. We know the rules."

The next day John Kennedy invited his brother and John Seigenthaler to breakfast at his Georgetown home. JFK began the discussion as his guests were served their bacon and eggs.

"Okay, Ribicoff turned me down."

"Why?"

"He said it wouldn't be politically wise to have a Catholic president and a Jewish attorney general pushing Negro civil rights issues on a Protestant South."

"I should have had him write my speech," Bobby said.

John looked at his brother and chose his words carefully. "Bobby, I've put together a very talented cabinet. The problem is I don't really know them. I don't know how much I can depend on their judgement, how straight they'll be with me."

Bobby and Seigenthaler nodded, but said nothing. The president continued. "I need someone whom I can trust, Bobby. Someone whose personal interests will not color his judgement. Someone who will never be afraid to tell me the truth. You're the only guy who fills the bill."

Bobby winked at Seigenthaler. "Here it comes. He's winding up for the pitch."

"Bobby, be serious. If I can ask Adlai Stevenson to make a sacrifice he doesn't want to make, if I can ask Bob McNamara to leave running Ford Motors for Defense, then certainly I can expect no less from my own brother. I need you in this government."

Jack poured himself another cup of coffee and gave Bobby a chance to think. After a moment Bobby spoke up.

"The fact that I made headlines fighting crime

on Senate subcommittees doesn't exactly qualify me for the highest law-enforcement position in the country."

JFK asked Seigenthaler for his opinion. Seigenthaler raised his hands, looked at Bobby, and said, "It appears that the ship of state has sailed and that you're on it."

John Kennedy pointed his fork at his brother. "I'm prepared to take the hail of criticism that you're too young, too inexperienced, and my brother. But all that resistance will dissolve when they see the job you'll do. Just watch."

Bobby shrugged and grinned. "Yes, Mr. President. But I don't know how you can announce it without creating a storm of controversy even before your inauguration."

"Well," said Jack, "one night about two A.M. I'll open the door, look up and down the street, and if there's no one around I'll whisper, 'It's Bobby!' And later I'll tell the press you need a little experience as attorney general before you go out and practice law."

Jack laughed and passed the biscuits.

CHAPTER 5

"That was the nicest inauguration you've ever taken me to." Jackie Kennedy put her arms around her husband and kissed him tenderly. It was 3:45 A.M., and the couple stood alone in the White House garden, a pale moon overhead. They walked arm in arm to the Oval Office portico. Within, the room was lit by a single green-shaded lamp. All was quiet. Their noses to the windows, they looked in.

Jackie nudged Jack. "I've found you the perfect desk."

"Now hold on, Jackie . . ."

"It didn't cost a cent. I found it in the White House basement."

"What's the matter with the one in there now?"

"It isn't you. Wait till you see the one I found.

It was a gift from Queen Victoria. It just needs refinishing. It's so you! It's made from timber from the HMS *Resolute*. Isn't that incredible?"

"Jackie . . ."

"Oh, Jack, this house could be so beautiful, but it's been so neglected. I want to restore it to the national treasure that it should be."

He gave her a hug. "Jackie, the taxpayers don't care about old timbers and fancy furniture. All they care about is . . ."

She danced away from him. "I've already thought about that. It won't cost the taxpayers a cent."

A few days after the inauguration, Harris Wofford was sitting in the president's outer office, talking to JFK's secretary, Evelyn Lincoln, when a short and very proper looking man walked in, holding a Bible. He approached Wofford and came right to the point.

"Is your name Harris Wofford?"

"Yes, it is. But who are you?"

"My name's Godbold. I'm here to swear you in. Raise your right hand."

"There must be some mistake. Are you sure you have the right Wofford?"

"I'm sure," replied Godbold, "you're the one. The president has ordered me to swear you in."

"Why?"

"It's not my job to question the president.

I'm here to swear you in, and the president wants it done immediately. Please cooperate. Repeat after me. I . . . state your name . . ."

"I, Harris Wofford . . ."

"Do solemnly swear and affirm that I will support and defend the office of the United States against all enemies, foreign and domestic, and that I will bear Truth, Faith, and Allegiance to the same, that I take this obligation freely without any mental reservation or purpose of evasion, and that I will well and faithfully discharge the duties of the office which I am about to enter, so help me God."

The swearing in over, Godbold turned on his heels and left. Thoroughly confused, Wofford looked toward the door to the Oval Office, where John F. Kennedy stood looking back at him, a smile on his lips. "Come in, Harris," said the president.

They were alone. John Kennedy sat behind his desk, indicating a hard-backed chair for Wofford, who sat down and looked at his hands. "I was just sworn in."

"Yes, I know."

"May I know what for, Jack?"

"I couldn't afford to lose you," said the president matter-of-factly. "I need an assistant for civil rights in the White House, someone who is respected by the Negro leaders. And that's you. You were one of those men who introduced Dr. King to the idea of nonviolent resistance as

41

practiced by Gandhi. So, now you can help keep the Negroes nonviolent while we work on these civil rights problems."

Wofford was still bewildered. "But Jack, I'm already working with Sargent Shriver, putting together the Peace Corps . . ."

"You can work on the Peace Corps in your spare time." JFK picked up a manila envelope and took out a thick file. "These figures in your report are shocking. They are more than shocking; they're a disgrace." Kennedy read the figures.

". . . only fifteen Negroes out of thirty-five hundred officers in the Foreign Service . . . of the nine hundred and fifty Justice Department lawyers, ten are Negroes . . . the Defense Department: four hundred Negroes out of seventy thousand employees . . . it goes on and on. Harris, we can change this *without* going through Congress."

Wofford was back on firm ground. "By setting up a strong presidential committee on equal employment you can require companies with government contracts to employ more Negroes."

As he spoke the door opened, and Bobby Kennedy strode in carrying several folders. He sat beside Wofford and they nodded their greetings. Jack Kennedy never missed a beat.

"Then you're going to stay on and help us make this work?"

"It would be an honor."

When Bobby spoke up there was a mischievous twinkle in his eye. "Jack, you sure you want this guy around? J. Edgar Hoover thinks he's a dangerous character." He slid a file onto his brother's desk. JFK read it and looked at Wofford.

"The FBI says you've been having phone conversations with a 'known Communist,' Harris. A man named Levison." The president handed Wofford the file. "What about all these phone calls?"

Wofford studied the file. "These dates are a few years ago. . . Why, these are Martin Luther King's phone numbers. I remember now. Stan Levison. He works with King. He always seemed more like a businessman than a Communist."

Jack Kennedy smiled. "Harris, talk to Dave and get yourself an office. We've got a lot of work to do."

When Wofford had gone, the brothers put their heads together. Bobby dumped the rest of the files on Jack's desk. "Well," he said, "according to Hoover's report, Wofford has two more strikes against him. He was the first white student to graduate from a black college. That alone is enough to get on Hoover's blacklist. And then he went to Yale Law School, which, for Edgar, is probably just as bad."

Jack thumbed through the files. "Hoover's already called me a few times. I've referred him to you."

"He's probably foaming at the mouth, Jack. He's never had to deal with a mere attorney general before, let alone the president's kid brother."

Jack grinned. "I was hoping you and he would become friends."

"*Friends!* That's very funny. Aside from being a pompous bigot, he exploits his position by collecting and leaking unsavory information about important people."

"Precisely, Bobby. I was counting on you to find out what he has in the files on us."

"Us?"

"Okay, me."

"The man is dangerous, Jack."

"Look, he'll only be around for my first term, period. On the first of January, 1965, he'll be seventy; time to retire. Anyway . . . here's the game plan: You're the bad guy, you try to keep him under control."

Bobby stood up to his full height, five feet nine and one half inches, and smiled.

"And let me guess, Mr. President. You're the good guy."

"You got it. Now just try to avoid any direct confrontations with him that could affect our programs in Congress."

"Right."

Jack rapped his knuckles on another folder. "Now, how about this? How are you going to explain to Dad that I'm not going to appoint his best friend a judge?"

"*Me* explain?"

* * *

It was one of the most awful moments of Miss Helen Gandy's life. She steadied herself. Taking a firm grip on the doorknob, she turned it and let herself into her boss's office. J. Edgar Hoover, who had said he was not to be disturbed, looked up from his memoirs and glowered at her.

"I . . . I'm . . . very sorry, Mr. Hoover," she stammered.

"Speak up, Miss Gandy!" the old man bellowed.

"Sir, I have spoken several times with President Kennedy's secretary, Mrs. Lincoln, and I've also spoken to his appointment secretary, Mr. O'Donnell, about your appointment with the president . . ."

Miss Gandy paused and took a deep breath, then exhaled.

"They both said . . . I mean suggested . . . that you call the attorney general."

"*What?*"

"Sir, Mr. Hoover, I told them that you were accustomed to dealing directly with the president, but . . . oh, sir, there must be some misunderstanding, I'm certain of it . . ."

Hoover looked like he was about to boil over. Miss Gandy fled.

Bobby Kennedy and John Seigenthaler, their shirtsleeves rolled up and their ties pulled loose, strode purposefully through the traffic in the Justice Department corridor, followed by Bobby's dog Brumus. They entered a small office on the fourth floor where a receptionist greeted them with a timid smile. Bobby held out his hand.

"Hello, I'm Bob Kennedy. What's your name?"

"Rose."

Bobby smiled. "That's my mother's name."

"I know, sir."

"Who works in here with you?"

"Mr. Robert Blakey, a lawyer in the Criminal Division."

At that moment Blakey appeared through a side door. "Mr. Attorney General, I'm Robert Blakey." He looked worried, darting his eyes from Kennedy to Seigenthaler. "We weren't expecting you. Is anything wrong?"

Bobby shook hands, then folded his arms. "Not at all. This is John Seigenthaler, my aide, and that's Brumus, my dog. We're just trying to get to know everybody around here. I just want to let you know that we are very interested in you and what you're doing, and that we want to hear about your problems or suggestions. My door is open; if I'm not around talk to John here."

"Thank you, sir."

Bobby lunged at Brumus, who was attacking a brown paper bag. "Get your nose outta there, boy! That's Rose's lunch!"

Ten minutes later, in Bobby's office, a round table had assembled, which included Bobby, Seigenthaler, Burke Marshall, Byron White,

Nicholas Katzenbach and John Doar. Bobby's secretary, Angie Novello, handed each of them a folder and left. Bobby was the first to speak.

"Gentlemen, since any new legislation is out of the question for now, we've got to enforce what's already on the books. This is not the Eisenhower administration. This attorney general *has* the support of the administration."

John Doar had a question. "What about forcing the states to show us their voter registration records? They've been ducking us for years."

"All right," said the attorney general.

Whizzer White was next. "Reverend King was pressing us last summer at the convention to provide more federal protection for civil rights workers."

"We should protect them," Bobby said emphatically.

"How can we do that?" Marshall asked. "We don't have a national police force, and we don't want one."

John Seigenthaler cautioned: "The FBI is too dependent on those southern sheriffs to make waves, and Mr. Hoover is too cozy with southern congressmen who support his appropriation bills every year."

Bobby looked at the group and smiled. "Why in *hell* did Jack reappoint him?"

Angie Novello entered and whispered to Bobby, "Mr. Hoover is still 'unavailable.'"

"What do I have to do to get the man on the phone?"

"Hey, Bobby," said Burke Marshall with a grin, "why don't you just walk over there? You're both on the same floor."

Bobby had his tongue in his cheek. "Are you seriously suggesting that the attorney general walk the five hundred yards of the fifth floor that it takes to get to his office?"

"Okay, then why don't you put in a direct line—office to office?"

Bobby looked at Angie and said, "Do it."

CHAPTER 6

Eight men sat around an oblong table in a suite at the Mayflower Hotel in Washington, D.C. Bobby Kennedy was on one side with his aides Burke Marshall, Louis Martin, and Harris Wofford. Facing them were the Reverends King and Abernathy, Roy Wilkins, and Stanley Levison. There were hors d'oeuvres and a large fruit salad, but no one was hungry, especially after the attorney general began the meeting with an apology.

"I know this is going to disappoint you," said Bobby, looking directly at Martin Luther King, "but we are not going to ask for the civil rights legislation that we promised you in the campaign. Not now."

Abernathy looked disgusted. "That disappoints me, but it doesn't surprise me." He looked at King. "Nothing's changed. We're still on our own."

Bobby spoke up. "A lot has changed. We're going to take executive action where we can move without Congress."

"What kind of action?" Wilkins wanted to know.

"Like employing Negroes in the government," Bobby replied. "And for the next four years we want to go all out, working with your people to get the right to vote for every Negro in America."

"That's the way for you to change things," Harris Wofford explained. "First you get the right to vote, then you elect Negroes to public office, and send friends of civil rights to Congress."

Burke Marshall added, "We'll do everything in our power to help you to get the Negro registered to vote, both in the South and the North."

Abernathy and King exchanged glances. Abernathy smiled and said, "Gentlemen, unlike the government, the civil rights movement is made up of . . . dedicated, strong-willed people who . . ."

When Abernathy paused to search for a word, Louis Martin jumped in. "Are you saying we're not as dedicated and stubborn as you?" he asked with a smile.

"No," said Reverend King. "He's saying Uncle Sam doesn't give us a payroll check every week.

To survive we depend on donations from a lot of different people."

"Half the time there's enough money for the rent or the phone bill," said Stanley Levison, "but not both."

King continued, "The point is that people who work with us have their own ideas about how to change racism and segregation."

"If y'all don't mind," said Abernathy, leaning back in his chair, "my point was that we're not organized like the government. We're made up of various 'governments'—the NAACP, the Congress for Racial Equality, the Southern Christian Leadership Conference, to mention just a few. Each has its own agenda."

"It's true," said Wilkins. "We try to unify what is to be done. We try to modify the extreme ideas and encourage the sensible ones. But, the fact is, with all due respect to Reverend King, there really is no 'boss' to the civil rights movement."

King looked at Kennedy. "I'm very unhappy to hear that you and your brother have decided not to go to Congress for the legislation you promised," he said.

"The election's over," said Abernathy. "They won."

". . . With the help of Negro voters," said Martin. "We know that. We have a special responsibility to the movement. We acknowledge that."

"Correct," asserted Harris Wofford. "The

only change we're talking about is strategy: what to do that will meet the least resistance and, at the same time, achieve the most significant change. That's how we decided to put all the government's power into getting Negroes registered to vote."

There was a silence while everyone looked at King.

"Naturally," King said, scanning the table, "we will work with you to achieve that goal. But we will need a lot of help."

Bobby nodded. "The president and I will give you full public support," he said. "Behind the scenes we'll help get you the money to do it."

"We'll need more than money, Mr. Kennedy," said King. "Negro registration in the South will be dangerous. We'll need protection, and that means help from the FBI."

The attorney general winced. "You know the problem with Mr. Hoover . . ."

"I do," King replied.

"Reverend King, I'll do the best I can."

On that note, the meeting ended.

Two days later, at 10:15 in the morning, Brumus loped down a corridor of the Justice Department and crossed the path of J. Edgar Hoover, who was on his way to work.

"Get that dog out of here immediately," he said to Clyde Tolson.

Tolson spoke carefully. "I can't, Mr. Hoover. It belongs to the attorney general."

Hoover snapped, "Have the GSA send him a memo to leave his animals home."

"Yessir."

That afternoon Bobby Kennedy returned from lunch and found something new on his desk—a black phone with no dial. He put down the newspapers and files he was carrying and picked up the phone. Miss Gandy answered.

"Let me speak with Mr. Hoover, please."

"I'm sorry, Mr. Attorney General," stammered Helen Gandy, "b-but Mr. Hoover is in a meeting right now and . . ."

Bobby broke in. "The purpose of this line, Miss Gandy, is to permit Mr. Hoover and me to communicate with one another without having to go through any other . . . bodies. Does he understand that?"

"I—I'm quite certain that Mr. Hoover is aware of your purpose in having the phone installed, Mr. Attorney . . ."

Bobby cut in again. ". . . Just a minute, Miss Gandy. Is this phone on his desk or yours?"

"It's . . . on my desk, but . . ."

The attorney general's voice turned to ice. "The next time I pick up this phone I only want to hear Mr. Hoover's voice and nobody else's. Is that clear?"

He hung up calmly but firmly.

One hour later J. Edgar Hoover, turning several shades of red, watched a telephone repairman install the hated black phone on his desk. No sooner had the workman left than the phone rang. It was Bobby, inviting the FBI chief over to his office for a 'friendly chat.'"

"Right now?" asked Hoover.

"Right now," said Kennedy.

Feet up on his desk, Bobby was throwing darts at a board nailed to a wood-paneled wall when Hoover and Tolson walked in. Hoover looked at the holes made by the darts in the oak paneling and winced. Bobby got right to the point.

"Edgar," he said, handing him a folder, "the two most important matters on my agenda are civil rights and organized crime."

"Organized crime." Hoover mouthed the words as if they were new.

"In that folder is a list of forty-seven crime bosses all over the U.S."

Hoover smiled at Tolson, looked back at Kennedy. "You mean hoodlums, thugs, bank robbers? We know about most of them. Certainly there are rings of car thieves operating across various state lines, but 'organized crime'? No, Bobby, I'm afraid that doesn't exist."

Bobby was baffled. "You haven't looked at the material we've developed, Edgar. It's in that folder."

Hoover placed the folder carefully on a thick stack of material on Tolson's lap and shrugged. "Bob, I've served five presidents before your brother. I've had this job for thirty-six years. I don't need you to . . ."

Bobby sprang to his feet. "Do you remember something called the McClellan Committee? I was on that committee, Edgar. We turned up concrete evidence that organized crime is a fact of American life! Before that there was Senator Kefauver's committee."

"I remember well how the committee created the myth of the 'Mafia' to get a lot of space in newspapers and magazines," said Hoover calmly.

Bobby was furious but controlled. "Now Edgar, fifty-five gangland leaders from all over the country met at Apalachin, New York, three years ago. You must have heard about it. Illegal gambling profits of seven billion dollars a year are used to bankroll narcotics, loansharking, white slavery, and bribery of police, judges, senators and congressmen!"

Again Hoover smiled. "I know those theories were contained in that book you wrote, Bob, but that doesn't make them facts."

"Why is it, Edgar, that the Bureau of Narcotics has more information on organized crime than the FBI? Now that is a fact!"

"I've seen no such information," Hoover replied.

Bobby was outwardly calm, but his knuckles were white. "I suggest that you read that file on organized crime, Edgar! And we will have a meeting on it, and we will discuss it in detail."

Hoover and Tolson rose and headed for the door. On their way Bobby called out, "Oh, Edgar? Of the five or six thousand agents we've got on the FBI payroll, how many are Negroes?"

Hoover spun around. "I don't know. We don't keep track of that information. We hire strictly on merit. You find me a Negro with the same qualifications as a white man and we'll hire him."

"Find out, please," said Bobby. The smile had returned to his face.

CHAPTER 7

The Reverend Martin Luther King lay in bed in a darkened motel room on the outskirts of Macon, Georgia, watching the ten o'clock news. As the announcer presented the details of the fiasco at Cuba's Bay of Pigs, King, like the rest of the country, was stunned.

. . . Once heralded as a hero by the United States government, Fidel Castro turned into a "dangerous dictator," one that was assumed to be a threat to the peace of the Americans. The secret invasion of Cuba was planned by expatriates from Cuba with the financial, technical, and tactical support of the Central Intelligence Agency and the American Armed Forces.

King was exhausted, but he kept himself

awake, trying to fathom the implications of the newscaster's words.

> . . . Hundreds of millions of dollars later, at dawn on the morning of April 16, the invasion began. Less than forty-eight hours later President Kennedy received the message that the invasion of Cuba was completely crushed by Castro's forces, resulting in the death or capture of over eleven hundred would-be liberators.

There was a knock at the door, then the voice of Clarence Jones, King's attorney, calling him. In his skivvies and robe, King got out of bed, turned off the television, and opened the door.

"Martin, I've got the final draft of your speech. Can I come in?"

King glanced back into the room. On the bed, wearing a white lace peignoir and brushing her hair, was a young and very attractive black woman. King turned back.

"Uh, Clarence, why don't we meet in your room in about an hour?"

Jones smiled. "Oh. You've got company."

"Yes."

Jones nodded. "It's all right, Martin. When you're on the road twenty-nine days out of thirty, with all the pressure, I guess you need some tender loving care."

"It doesn't mean I love my family any less," King said defensively.

"Of course not," Jones replied. "I understand."

The two men hugged. Jones left.

Bobby Kennedy and John Seigenthaler were in Bobby's office when Courtney Evans, a short, shy, and precise man of forty-two, was announced. Evans, who had served as FBI liaison with Kennedy in the rackets committee days, continued that role in the Department of Justice. He looked concerned.

"Bobby, I'm not here officially, but off the record there's a time bomb ticking in Hoover's office."

Bobby and Seigenthaler exchanged an amused look.

"Do we have any idea who put it there, Courtney?" Bobby asked innocently.

"I wish it were funny. The time bomb is Mr. Hoover. I can't begin to tell you how infuriated he is that he has been unable to speak with the president. It's been blown way out of proportion."

"He hasn't mentioned it to me," said Bobby.

"He used to have lunch regularly with all the other presidents."

"Not with Truman," Seigenthaler pointed out. Evans ignored him.

"Bobby, if there is anything you could do, it would help enormously to repair what I'm afraid is a very destructive situation. But don't mention my name, please."

Bobby thought for a moment, then picked up the black phone without a dial. Hoover answered on the fifth ring, an edge to his voice. Bobby's tone was friendly.

"Hello, Edgar? How are you this fine day? Wonderful. Edgar, the president has asked me to tell you that he'll be happy to have you join him for lunch at the White House next Thursday at one-fifteen. Yes, Edgar. No, I won't be there; just you and the president. Certainly. Good-bye, Edgar."

Evans was relieved. "Thank you, Bobby. As I said before, please don't mention my name . . ."

When Evans had left, Bobby turned to Seigenthaler. "Now, maybe we'll get some cooperation . . ."

Fifteen minutes later Courtney Evans was seated at the conference table in Hoover's office. Hoover's top assistant, William Sullivan—short, well-built, and eager to please—sat at Hoover's left, Clyde Tolson on his right. Several other FBI supervisors filled the table. Sam Noisette, in a black suit and tie, served coffee. Hoover pointed a thick finger at Evans.

"Now that you're the new liaison to the attorney general I expect to see weekly written reports."

"Sir?"

"I want written reports covering everything Kennedy says and plans to do. You will tell him nothing about our activities. Period."

"Yessir."

"I want you to work with Al Rosen in Civil Rights and Sullivan here in National Security."

"Yessir."

The black phone on Hoover's desk rang. He let it ring. The other men in the room pretended not to notice. Hoover let the phone ring five times, then it stopped. Tolson handed the director a folder. Hoover glanced at it, handed it to Sullivan.

"Bill, I'm promoting you. You're the new assistant director of security, a very important position now that Kennedy and his Ivy League punks are going to screw up everything."

"Thank you very much, Mr. Hoover," said Sullivan. "I won't disappoint you."

The meeting was adjourned.

James Farmer, head of the Congress of Racial Equality, was a man who believed that action, not talk, got things done. He believed he had been doing too much talking, and he knew he was talking too much now. But here he was, as promised, in the Department of Justice, facing the attorney general, whom he had never met, speaking his mind.

"I know what the Supreme Court has said, Mr. Kennedy. That there shall be no segregation in bus terminals involved with interstate commerce, but we all know how meaningless that is."

Martin Luther King spoke up. "Nothing's changed out there, Mr. Attorney General. Separate toilets, separate drinking fountains, just like it's always been. If you're black you can't sit down for a cup of coffee."

Farmer felt his anger getting the best of him. "The bus companies either can't read or they don't give a damn about what the Supreme Court decides."

Bobby spoke calmly. "Time, gentlemen, that's all we're asking for. You've got to understand that the Interstate Commerce Commission is a very independent, very slow-moving agency. We're working on them. I assure you, but it takes time."

At that moment the intercom on Bobby's desk buzzed. It was his secretary asking him to take a call. He picked up a telephone and listened; then he stood up and apologized. "Gentlemen, I'll be with you in one minute."

After he had left the office, Farmer glared at King. "I told you talking doesn't work. Martin, we've got to put pressure on these people. We've got to create a crisis, something big and bold that will get us coverage in the newspapers and TV. Then they'll do something!"

Bobby returned, sat down at his desk. "Now, gentlemen, where were we?"

Bobby Kennedy didn't know it, but the time to talk was over, and the time to wait was running out.

* * *

Less than a week later in the Atlanta office of the Southern Christian Leadership Conference, King, Abernathy, and Farmer, wearing overalls, sat around a table studying a highway map of the southeastern U.S. Around them a dozen black volunteers manned typewriters and telephones in a flurry of activity that James Farmer liked. Suddenly the room grew still. On television, high in one corner of the room, Jack Kennedy looked boldly into the camera and spoke: ". . . I take full responsibility for the 'Bay of Pigs' invasion and fiasco which resulted in 1,131 men taken prisoner by Fidel Castro's troops. I promise that I will secure freedom for those brave men who are being held prisoner—regardless of the price."

Ralph Abernathy snapped off the TV. "How come Kennedy's so worked up about freedom for those Cubans? We're Americans, and we've been prisoners here for hundreds of years! And nobody gives a damn!"

The phone rang. It was for Farmer. He listened briefly, hung up, and pointed to the map. "Okay, it's begun."

A cheer went up around the office. When it died down, Farmer spoke loud enough for everyone to hear. "The Freedom Ride buses are almost out of Georgia. We expect the first of the two buses to reach Anniston, Alabama, tomorrow morning. The second bus goes directly into Birmingham. The Alabama State Highway Patrol has promised them protection."

"How much is that promise worth?" King asked.

"It's all we've got," said Abernathy. "The Justice Department has not responded to our request for protection."

"When do they get to Birmingham?" someone demanded.

"Tomorrow night!" shouted Farmer.

King took his friend aside. "The night's a dangerous time, Jim. We could at least arrange to have them arrive in the daylight."

Farmer shook his head. "They understand that they are risking their lives, Martin. They discussed among themselves that if the buses break down they'll walk all the way to New Orleans. Nothing's going to stop them, nothing's going to slow them down."

"I just pray that no one gets hurt," said Martin Luther King.

At eight o'clock the following morning Gary Thomas Rowe, a big, muscular, crew-cut man in his mid thirties, stood beside his car on a country road outside Birmingham, Alabama. He lit a cigarette, smoked it, and lit another. A black Plymouth approached and stopped. The driver, an FBI agent, got out and walked up to Rowe. While they talked, Rowe put a jack on his rear bumper and went through the motions of changing a tire. While he worked he talked to the agent over his shoulder.

"Y'all bring the cash?"

The agent produced a white envelope and handed it to Rowe, who opened it, counted the money, and stuffed it all in his back pocket.

"I guess it's all there," he said.

"The FBI always pays well for the right information."

Rowe looked around, then spoke softly. "Okay, here's the story. You know Bull Connor?"

The agent nodded. "Eugene Connor, commissioner of the Birmingham police . . ."

"You got it. Well, yesterday Bull had a drink with the head man of the Klan. Seems there's a busload of niggers and nigger lovers coming to Birmingham tomorrow."

"We know all about that."

"Yeah, but what you don't know is this: Bull Connor's promised the Klan they can beat the people on that bus to a bloody pulp. He's giving them twenty minutes to do whatever they want before he sends the police in."

"Are you sure of this, Rowe?"

"They made the announcement at last night's meeting." Rowe smiled and stepped aside so the agent could see inside the trunk. In it were several lengths of chain, two baseball bats, a pickhandle, a case of Budweiser beer and a stiff white sheet.

The agent handed Rowe a piece of paper.

"What's this?"

"It's a receipt for the money I just gave you. Sign it."

Rowe had to borrow a pen. He signed the receipt, got in his car, and drove off.

That same day, Saturday, well before noon, three FBI agents were hard at work laying new sod, pruning, planting, and fertilizing the garden in J. Edgar Hoover's backyard. Supervised by their boss, Hoover himself, the men worked in silence. Clyde Tolson appeared, said something to Hoover, and the two men huddled in the far end of the garden. Out of earshot, the agents muttered as they worked.

"Bad enough we have to do ten hours of 'voluntary' overtime during the week, but Saturday is too much!" said one. "Why should he get his garden done for nothing? My wife's sore as hell about our having to pay for all this, too—from what's supposed to be the FBI recreation fund."

"Shhh!" said the other. "He's looking this way! You be careful or we'll be transferred to Butte, Montana, tomorrow."

At the other end of the garden Clyde Tolson spoke even more softly. "Excuse the interruption, Mr. Hoover, but I thought you'd better know this right away. An Alabama informant of ours just told the Birmingham office that Bull Connor will give the Ku Klux Klan twenty minutes to work over the Freedom Riders before he steps in."

Hoover nodded.

"Shall I inform the attorney general?"

"No."

CHAPTER 8

Bobby was with Jack in the Oval Office when the news came over the radio. The brothers listened in silence.

. . . Unaware that the tires of their bus had been slashed before they left Atlanta, the Freedom Riders found themselves stalled on the side of the road near Anniston, Alabama. It was here they were attacked by several truckloads of whites who had been following the bus.

Had it not been for an Alabama State Highway Patrolman who was on board the bus, the Freedom Riders would certainly have been badly beaten. The Patrolman, who stated to reporters that he was personally opposed to desegregation, nonetheless defended the bus passengers. However, the group of violent whites came armed with pipes and clubs and succeeded in burning the bus.

The Freedom Riders that arrived in Birmingham weren't as lucky. A mob of whites viciously attacked them without the intervention of the local police. When queried, Birmingham Chief of Police 'Bull' Connor claimed that since it was Mother's Day he had given most of his men the day off.

The president and the attorney general looked at Harris Wofford. Bobby threw up his hands. "Why wasn't I told about these 'Freedom Riders'? Where were the Alabama police? Why didn't the FBI know?"

Wofford was not about to take the blame. "I knew about it," he said, "and so did you. We both got the same memo from the SCLC."

John Kennedy was firm. "Put a stop to it, Bobby. We agreed to focus our efforts on the right to vote. We didn't say anything about bus terminals."

"Nobody can stop them now, Mr. President," said Wofford.

"Look," said the president, "I'm about to have my first meeting with Khrushchev. It sure would be appreciated, Bobby, if there were no sit-ins, protest marches, or bombings while it was going on."

Bobby gave orders. "Harris, tell Seigenthaler and Doar to get down to Birmingham fast. We've got to give those people some protection."

When Wofford had gone, Bobby shook his head. "How is this going to look to the rest of the world?"

"Like we're a bunch of barbarians," the president was quick to reply. Then, just as quickly, he changed the subject. "Something else I'd like you to concentrate on is figuring out a way to get the Bay of Pigs prisoners released by Castro."

"We're working on it, Jack."

Jack sighed. "That's what everybody tells me."

"I'm not everybody," snapped his brother. "Look, what about the executive order against discrimination in federally assisted housing? When are you going to sign it?"

"In due time."

"Jack, the NAACP is going to press you hard on that one. How about Reverend King? When are you going to see him? It's been . . ."

"Are you sure you're not on his payroll?" The president winked.

Late that night, in his Justice Department office, Bobby, his secretary, and Harris Wofford manned the telephones.

"Bobby, line four," said Angie Novello. "It's the Greyhound Bus Company. Nobody wants to drive the bus from Birmingham to Montgomery."

Bobby grabbed the phone. "How many drivers do you have? Two thousand? Do you mean to say you can't get one of them to drive that bus?"

Wofford held up another phone. "It's Martin King."

"Dr. King? I know . . . yes, I've heard. Listen, Dr. King, I can see only one way to stop this bloodshed. You've got to get Farmer to call off the Freedom Rides. If you'll do that I'll try my damnedest to get Governor Patterson and the other southern governors to totally desegregate their bus stations. Yes? But . . . yes, I see. Very well . . ."

Bobby said good-bye and handed the phone to Harris Wofford. "He wouldn't go for it, Harris."

"It's just as well," said Wofford. "You never could have gotten Patterson to agree. He's for segregation now and forever."

Bobby Kennedy was tired. He put his head in his hands, rubbed his eyes. Then he picked up the phone and dialed.

"Alabama State Police? This is Robert Kennedy . . ."

Courtney Evans made his weekly report to J. Edgar Hoover when they were alone in the director's office.

"The attorney general was . . . wondering, sir, about what stopped the FBI agents in Birmingham from protecting the Freedom Riders from the mob. He said all our agents did was take notes and make a film record of the event— while these people were getting clubbed."

Hoover spat out his words. "You tell that punk to check the name of this organization! We're the Federal Bureau of *Investigation*. Tell him to look up 'investigation' in the dictionary, if he's got one. We're not cops! We investigate!"

"Ah, sir, the attorney general would like to know who the informant was who tipped off the Bureau . . ."

"You tell him we never reveal the names of our informants, never!"

Ten minutes later Evans stood before Bobby's desk.

"Sir, Mr. Hoover shares your distress at the shameful conduct and neglect of the Birmingham police, whose job it was to protect the bus riders. He asks that I point out to you that the FBI's mandate, as you doubtless recall, is to investigate . . ."

"Did you get the name of the informant?"

"Ah, T-37, sir."

"Who's T-37?"

"All our informants are given code names . . ."

"I don't want his code name, I want his real name!"

"Yes, sir. Mr. Hoover said he presumes you understand the FBI never reveals the identity of its informants. If we did they wouldn't live very long."

Kennedy took a deep breath and counted to ten. Then,

"Okay. Now we're going to talk about organized crime."

"Sir?"

"Tell Mr. Hoover . . . that I want an immediate reply on the organized crime file we presented to him two weeks ago. Tell him he's not squirming out of this one. I've introduced two anticrime bills that specifically put organized crime in his lap. Tell him I said if the FBI doesn't have time to deal with it I'll set up a new agency!"

When Evans delivered the message Hoover laughed.

"Tell him he's dreaming! He's trying to get the FBI to deal with his childish nightmares and fantasies. There's no such thing as organized crime!"

"Yes, sir."

"Do you agree?"

"Sir, that file contains some . . ."

"I don't give a damn about that file! Do you agree with me or not?"

"I do, sir."

"All right. Now you tell that fool that if he wishes to set up a new department to do investigative work that is rightfully that of the FBI . . . tell him I'll retire tomorrow!"

Evans retraced his steps to Bobby's office, and in his most politic manner presented the ultimatum. Bobby sat back in his chair.

"What are you trying to say, Courtney?"

"Mr. Hoover said he would be very . . . disappointed if you were to create a new department to investigate organized crime."

"I got that. What did he say about quitting?"

"Ah, he said something about his pension being due . . ."

"He said he'd quit if I set up a separate agency?"

"I, ah, suppose that's one way of looking at it, sir."

Bobby Kennedy smiled. "Tell him I said that would be *fantastic!*"

CHAPTER 9

On Friday, May 17, 1961, at 3:15 P.M., Burke Marshall entered a phone booth in Montgomery Airport and quickly dialed the attorney general.

"Bob? Uh, we've got a problem. Dr. King's plane will be here in an hour, the Freedom Rider bus will be at the Montgomery terminal in less than an hour, and so far, of the five hundred U.S. marshals Whizzer White ordered up, only fifty have shown."

Five minutes later, from a phone booth in the Montgomery bus terminal, John Doar dialed the same number.

"Bob! There are no police! Wait? We can't wait! The bus just pulled in! Bob, there's a mob of people standing around waiting for those doors to open. No, I've called the police. Seigenthaler's at the police station. Nothing's happened. Oh Jesus! They're opening the doors, the passengers are coming out! Bob, it's terrible! No, yes! They're beating the passengers with clubs and chains! Oh my God, there's blood everywhere . . ."

Doar hung up so that he could call for ambulances. Ten minutes later he placed another call to Robert Kennedy.

"Bob! Seigenthaler's been hit! I saw the whole thing. He got here by taxi, and as he was getting out a black girl, one of the passengers, came running at him. She was crying and covered with blood, Bob! Seigenthaler grabbed her and pushed her in the taxi, but while he was doing that two guys ran up behind him and clubbed him to the ground! No! He's still there! No! No, not a policeman in sight! No, the ambulances won't come. We've called the black ambulances . . ."

In his office in the Justice Department, Bobby Kennedy held two phones in his hands, John Doar on one line and Burke Marshall on the other. His hands were shaking, but his voice was firm.

"John? Whatever you do, do not hang up! Burke? Burke, our friend Governor Patterson has reneged on his deal. Yes, the Freedom Riders are getting clubbed at the bus station. Sure, I'd love to send the Army in there, but the South would react to that like it was the Civil War army of occupation. No, Burke, we're moving on this. We're getting injunctions against the KKK, the

National States' Rights party, and the Birmingham and Montgomery police!

"No! No, just stay there at the airport and wait for King. Call all the ambulances you can, even if you have to phone out of state. And listen, when King gets there keep him away from that bus station! No, get him directly to the church, the First Baptist, downtown Montgomery . . ."

That night, inside the battle-torn First Baptist Church the Reverend Martin Luther King placed his call to the Justice Department.

"Well, Mr. Attorney General, they've set fire to a car out front, and somebody just threw a brick through the window. Outside of that everything's okay . . ."

Kennedy's voice was flat, exhausted. "The first thing we do tomorrow is get those Freedom Riders out of jail."

"No," King insisted. "They must stay where they are. This is a question of principle and ethics. By remaining in jail, they become living demonstrations of what they believe."

"As much as I sympathize, Dr. King, their actions will not influence the course of action the government will follow. Unfortunately, their presence behind bars will not influence me either."

"Mr. Kennedy. When the Freedom Riders arrived in this city there were no police. The FBI did nothing but stand around taking notes. I'm not asking the law to make a man love me, but it can keep him from lynching me!"

Bobby Kennedy paused, then continued. "Dr. King . . . this must stop. We've got to have a cooling-off period so we can get behind voter registration, which is our agreed upon priority. You've got to stop the Freedom Riders . . ."

"No cooling off! Jim Abernathy says we've been cooling off for a hundred years and if we get any cooler we'll be in the freezer!"

"I understand that, but . . ."

"Mr. Attorney General, perhaps it would help if we got a couple of hundred thousand students from up North to come down here and protest."

"Threats are no way to deal with us, Dr. King."

King was losing his patience. "Threats? There are a thousand people outside this building trying to come in here and kill us! That's a threat! Sir . . . I am deeply appreciative of what the administration is doing. And I do see a ray of hope. But I feel the need of being free *now*."

King hung up.

J. Edgar Hoover and the ever-present Clyde Tolson had had a long day in the Justice Department and were headed home when Hoover spotted William Sullivan in the fifth-floor corridor.

"Bill," said the director in a hushed tone, "I've read that two-year-old report you sent me on this damn Martin Luther King. Very thin."

"Yessir."

"Is that all we've got on him?"

"At this point, sir . . ."

"King was involved with that Negro Communist Ben Davies. Did you know that?"

"I . . . uh . . . I'll put some men on it and see what we can find, sir."

"Excellent. By the way, Bill, I've taken some men from Security and moved them into Civil Rights."

"Sir?"

Hoover growled. "I want to show the attorney general that the FBI is on the job. We're ready to track down crime wherever it occurs!"

"Yes sir."

"Come along, Junior!"

Secret Service Agent Boggs, a meticulous man who took great pride in his work, had little time to think about civil rights Freedom Riders down South. Boggs was on a special assignment for the President, which was why he was in a Manhattan office building waiting for a certain person to come out of the elevator.

Judith Campbell, a young beauty with a fabulous figure, came out of the elevator carrying a briefcase and a pocketbook. For a moment she stood looking around nervously, until Boggs tapped her on the shoulder. She jumped.

"Good afternoon, Miss Campbell, it's me again."

". . . Good afternoon."

"If you'll just follow me, please."

She followed the agent into an underground passage which let her out in the Carlyle Hotel on Madison Avenue. Boggs waved good-bye to her. He almost smiled.

Half an hour later Judith Campbell, very scantily clad, was in the bedroom of an enormous suite, giving President John F. Kennedy a backrub.

"Hey, take it easy!" he said as she worked her fingers along his spine.

"I'm so sorry," she said. "Is that better?"

"Mmmmm."

"Does that hurt?"

"I can stand any pain as long as I know it's going to end."

"Jack, did you hear about the movie?"

Kennedy knew what was coming. He smiled. "What movie?"

"I was sure you'd heard about it. I read about it in two different magazines. I'm sure I got it right. Jerry Wald at Twentieth Century Fox is planning to make a movie based on your brother's book, *The Enemy Within*."

JFK laughed. "Bobby gets all the breaks. He'll probably replace me in the White House one day."

She removed her negligee and dropped it on the floor. "It would really be terrific if you could talk to your brother about it . . ."

"What about it?"

". . . about getting me a part in the movie. You know, just a small part."

Jack laughed and turned over on his back.

"What's so funny?" she demanded. "I can act."

"I'm sure you can. It's just that I don't have any pull with Bobby when it comes to things like literature and . . . art."

"You're making fun of me."

He kissed her. "After two years don't I have that privilege?"

She giggled. "I still haven't learned what to talk about . . . with a president. It would be so different if you were a singer, or an actor maybe."

"Listen, I'm only the son of a whiskey smuggler. Does that make it easier?"

She began to massage his chest. A moment passed, then, "Jack, there are whiskey smugglers and there are whiskey smugglers."

"You've known a few?"

"None like your father."

"Look, forget about Bobby's movie. It'll be mean and ugly and cold, all the things you're not. Save yourself for something beautiful."

"Like what?"

"Wait till I write my next book. When they make the movie you can be in that."

"Paul Newman is going to play your brother's part."

"My father's the one you should be massaging. He used to be a movie producer."

"You're putting me on again."

"Paul Newman? Are you sure?"

"Why Jack, you're jealous!"

He pulled her down to him.

CHAPTER 10

Miss Gandy took a letter.

"To all Special Agents in Charge of Field Offices," Hoover began. "Subject: excess weight. Three months from the above date you are to submit to this office a report listing the names of those agents who are overweight—including the number of excess pounds for such agents."

Sam Noisette entered noiselessly with coffee and cake, which he placed on Hoover's desk. When Hoover spotted it his mouth became a thin line.

"Get . . . that . . . cake . . . off . . . my . . . desk!"

Sam snatched up the cake. "Mr. Hoover, sir, you always have cheesecake at this time of day."

"Not any more!" he snapped. "Get it out of my sight!"

It was then that Hoover noticed Tolson standing beside him, almost at attention.

"What is it, Junior?"

Tolson started to speak, but checked himself. He looked at Helen Gandy. Hoover caught the look.

"You're excused, Miss Gandy."

When the secretary had gone Tolson produced a file he had been holding behind his back. Hoover read it quickly.

"Why, the man is insatiable!"

"One could ask," began Tolson, "how the man has time to run the country and . . . service that many women at the same time."

Hoover tapped the file. "I don't know, Clyde. Put more men on it at once."

"Yessir."

Hoover leaned back, looked at the ceiling. "The doctor gave me an A-OK, Junior. Just like last year."

"I presumed he would, sir."

The director pointed at his aide. "You mention a word of what I'm going to tell you to anyone and I'll ship you off to Alaska before you can say 'Jack's my uncle.'"

"Sir?"

"I'm a little overweight."

"Really? I never would have thought so . . ."

Hoover patted his stomach. "Not a lot. Just a little." He rubbed his forehead. "I'm going to lie down for a bit, Junior. See that I'm not disturbed."

Tolson picked up the file and left.

On the afternoon of December 15, 1961, Jack and Bobby Kennedy moved nervously about the covered furniture on the sunporch of their father's Palm Beach mansion. Their mood was as grim as the weather outside, where a northeast wind howled, full of spitting rain. Low gray scudding clouds hovered over an angry sea. They looked up when their father entered the room.

Joe Kennedy could feel the tension. "Well, boys," he said after shaking hands, "what's this all about?"

"Hoover sent me two memos yesterday," said Bobby. "They were transcripts of wiretapped conversations between Sam Giancana and John Roselli, two of the biggest crooks in Chicago."

"What's that have to do with me?"

"Both men referred to contributions they made to Jack's campaign."

John F. Kennedy was bewildered. "Why, Dad? You could have written a check for whatever sum we needed."

"I couldn't buy Illinois with all my money," snapped Joe. He smiled. "Boys, we got a lot of checks. Who remembers who they came from? Call the accountants."

"I remember that you had an understanding with Mayor Daley," said Jack. "I should have asked you then what it was, but I didn't."

"You didn't want to know at the time."

"You're right, Dad, I remember. But I want to know now. We both want to know. Christ, this is enough to blow me right out of office!"

Joe Kennedy put his hand on John's shoulder. "Even if it were true, son, the secret is safe with Hoover. He's an old friend. He doesn't want to destroy you. He merely wants to remain in office."

"What was the deal?" Bobby demanded. "What did you promise them? Did you promise them we'd go easy on them?"

"Lower your voice," said Joe, looking over his shoulder. "As I recall, we needed Illinois badly. But I made no specific promises."

A pained look stole across JFK's face. "Dad, on election night you said something to me that I found . . . curious."

"What was that?"

"You said that dealing with civil rights at home and keeping peace with Russia was a big enough bite for the president's first term. Then you said, 'Don't waste time fighting organized crime.'"

Bobby's eyes widened. "Now we know. That's it! Lay off Giancana, Roselli, and the rest of the Mafia, right? What about Marcello? Was there a check from him, too?"

"Son, I honestly don't remember who the checks were from. And even if I did, whose signatures do you think would be on them?"

"They are the enemy," said Bobby. "And I'm going after them."

"I know that, and may God help you do it," said his father.

"Why did you do it, Dad?" asked John. "Why did you do it?"

Joe Kennedy brought his hands together. "Without Illinois we would have lost, boys. That's all there is to it. Now, how about we all go in and have a drink?"

Back in Washington, D.C., Lyndon Johnson was having a Saturday lunch at the home of his friend and neighbor, J. Edgar Hoover. Hoover was eating cottage cheese and fruit, while Johnson sliced a thick steak. The only other person in the lavish dining room was "Special Agent" James Crawford, who waited for their plates to empty.

Johnson grinned. "You know, the President's Commission on Equal Employment Opportunities is something I enjoy running. We're going to make some big changes in the country before we're done."

"They're keeping you busy?"

"Well, no. Except for the Committee they keep me pretty much out in the cold."

"A man with your abilities?" Hoover smiled.

Johnson did not. "That's not funny, Edgar."

"Sorry."

Johnson looked at Hoover's cottage cheese. "How can you eat that stuff?"

"Oh," said Hoover, "it's not so bad. It's pretty good, actually. Once in a while."

Johnson cut a huge piece of steak, chewed and swallowed. "Anyway, I might as well have my office in Cairo or Houston for all the good it does me being in the White House. You'd think I had some kind of disease the way they go out of their way to be polite to me and, at the same time, keep me away from everything that's going on."

"What have you got to complain about?" asked Hoover. "I have to deal with the snot-nosed kid brother!"

"Edgar, you're only the director of the FBI. I'm the goddamn vice president of the United States, for Christ sake!"

"True," said Hoover, popping a strawberry in his mouth.

"Oh, I guess I shouldn't complain. They let me make a few announcements to the news people. For instance, I got to announce to the world that Specialist Four James Davis of Livingston, Tennessee, was killed by the Vietcong, making him the first American soldier to fall in defense of our freedom in Vietnam." Johnson shook his head. "And then there was another one: 'The troops in Vietnam have been told to fire if they have been fired upon.' That's the kind of crap they give me to entertain and startle the newsmen with."

Hoover laughed. "You're lucky, actually . . ."

"This ought to be good," said Johnson.

". . . President Kennedy could have said the Bay of Pigs was your idea."

Johnson glared. "Fortunately, I was out of the country when that royal screw-up occurred."

"I've never been out of the country," Hoover stated with pride.

"I know it. Hey, how about some of that great cheesecake you always have around?"

CHAPTER 11

Bill Sullivan yawned and poured himself another cup of coffee. It was night, his secretary had gone home, and he was alone in his office in the building across the street from the Justice Department when Burke Marshall walked in with a stack of memos under his arm. The FBI supervisor shook his hand warmly.

"What can I do for you, Burke?"

Marshall put the memos on Sullivan's desk. "I would have called for an appointment," he apologized, "but it's after five and all the intelligent people have gone home."

Sullivan offered him a seat and coffee. Marshall refused both politely. "Listen, Bill, these endless memos from your office about the 'apparent' Communist infiltration of the civil rights movement . . ."

"Yes?"

"They're all based on speculation, on hearsay statements from unidentified informants. Nothing personal, but it's mostly gossip and you know it."

Sullivan got up and closed his office door. Then he sat down again and leaned closer to Marshall. "You know, Burke, every couple of weeks I have this office checked for bugs. Does that surprise you?"

Marshall was surprised. "You're serious," he said quietly.

"Off the record, okay?" Sullivan specified. "I'm pretty sure my secretary is spying on me. That's not unusual, understand? That's the way things are here."

"I appreciate your candor," said Marshall.

"I can trust you, Burke. As far as the memos we crank out go, that is because we are required to crank them out and we will continue to crank them out."

"All because of Hoover's preoccupation with the Communists, right?"

"Right. And to feed and flatter his ego. We all do it."

Marshall shook his head and looked around the office. "Is Hoover burning the midnight oil, too?"

"Are you kidding?" Sullivan shot him a look of disgust. "He's on an inspection tour of the southern FBI offices. Know what that means? It means he and Tolson are winter vacationing in Florida so they can catch the racing season, which they do every year. In July they spend a month in La Jolla, courtesy of Clint Murchison, so they can attend the races at Del Mar."

"Hey, I could use a vacation."

"Listen, officially Tolson and Hoover *never* take vacations. We had an agent who made the mistake of telling them he hoped they had nice weather for their 'vacation.' He was fired before they got to the airport."

"What a tyrant."

"Burke, there's a story about a time when Tolson came to work depressed. Hoover showed him a list of all his supervisors, including me, and said, 'Pick somebody on the list and fire him. That'll make you feel better.'"

"How can you work in a place like this?"

"You know what keeps me going? I believe that the FBI could be a first-rate intelligence agency again, with the right person running it. I hang in because I hope that one day someone with enough power will realize that the FBI is going to fall apart if Hoover isn't retired. He was a good director, a great director, but he's stuck in the past, he just won't change. He should have quit years ago, when his real work was done."

Marshall heaved a sigh and walked to the door. He paused. "One last bit of candor, okay? The talk about Hoover and Tolson . . ."

"About their being homosexual? No. No proof has ever emerged. Mr. Hoover attributes it to two Communist disinformation agents. You know, the KGB."

Marshall thanked him and left. A moment later Agent Logan hurried in.

"What have you got?" Sullivan asked.

"I've learned an important lesson tonight. Thoroughness pays off like crazy."

"I'm tired, Logan. Let's hear it."

"Okay. The surveillance film I had reshot in Atlanta? Bingo! Two of King's close associates in the film are probable Communists. One of them is the biggie you know about—Stanley Levison. And now we've got another, Jack O'Dell."

Logan placed a thick file on Sullivan's desk. Fastened to it was a recent photograph of King's associate, Stanley Levison, and another of Jack O'Dell.

Sullivan raised his eyebrows. "Good work, Logan . . ."

"How's your father doing, Bobby?" Burke Marshall asked. It was another late night at the Justice Department, and the attorney general was dead tired and depressed. The workload was enormous and growing steadily, and now his father was in the hospital recuperating from a stroke.

"He's the same," Bobby replied wearily. "One side is paralyzed and he still can't talk, but he seems stronger."

Marshall waited a moment before handing him a file. While Bobby read it carefully, John Seigenthaler asked Marshall about the state of affairs in Albany, Georgia, the current target for civil rights activism. Marshall could not conceal his anger.

"On the telephone Mayor Kelley tells me he's willing and able to meet with responsible Negro leaders, but every time he holds a press conference, which is pretty often, he says that segregation is a way of life in Albany."

"My God," said Bobby, pointing to the file. "Great way to start 1962! According to J. Edgar, two known Communists, Stanley Levison and Jack O'Dell, are now working publicly with Martin Luther King."

Bobby moaned, then asked, "Who is 'Solo'?"

Courtney Evans spoke for the bureau. "Solo is a code name for an informant in the Communist party who has provided the bureau with reliable information for years."

"Damn it!" Robert Kennedy slammed the desk with his fist. "That's all we need now—to have the whole civil rights program labeled a Communist front!"

"Here's a memo from the director," said Evans, handing him another envelope. "Mr. Hoover requested that I deliver this to you personally. Mr. Hoover considers this a matter of the utmost urgency."

Bobby read the memo aloud. ". . . In the interest of national security the FBI urgently requests authorization from the attorney general to place phone taps on Levison's phones. Your signature will confirm such authorization . . . J. Edgar Hoover, Director."

Kennedy, Seigenthaler and Marshall exchanged looks. Then Bobby picked up a pen and signed. When he had finished, he flashed Seigenthaler a worried look.

"John, do you remember the Levison calls from King's office that are in Wofford's file? We've got to get word to King. Where's Harris Wofford?"

"I don't know."

"Find him. I'll talk to him about advising King. But the rest of you, find a way to tell King that he's got to get rid of Levison and this guy O'Dell fast. Hoover could leak their Communist connections whenever he likes."

"Unfortunately," said Seigenthaler, "we can't tell him about the telephone tap on Levison's phones."

Bobby pounded his desk again. "Damn it!"

CHAPTER 12

A few nights later Martin Luther King was in bed in a Mississippi motel room, watching television. He was not alone. A light-skinned and very pretty black woman named Janet lay beside him. It was a hot night, and she was completely nude.

"Hey, Martin . . ."

"Hold it, honey," said King, pointing to the TV. "Listen to this." On screen, John F. Kennedy was delivering his state of the union address.

. . . With the approval of this Congress we have undertaken in the past year a great new effort in outer space. Our aim is not simply to be the first on the moon, any more than Charles Lindbergh's real aim was to be the first to Paris. Our objective in making this effort, which we hope will place one of our citizens on the moon, is to develop a new frontier of science, commerce, and cooperation . . .

Janet went to the bathroom to get a glass of water. She stood with it in the doorway, her slender body silhouetted in the bright light. King lost interest in the TV, and listened when she spoke.

"Hey Martin, you know the president. How about arranging it so I can be the first citizen to go to the moon?"

King patted the bed beside him. "I don't think you should make the trip," he said.

"Why not?" she asked, sitting down.

"Well, first of all you'd have to sit in the back of the spaceship."

Janet picked up a pillow and flung it at him. Laughing heartily, he blocked it. He caught her arms and pulled her to him.

"Then, once you got to the moon, it would be just like in Texas, Virginia, Alabama, Arkansas, and right here in Mississippi. You'd have to pay your moon poll tax!"

"You're crazy."

"No, girl," he said, giving her bottom a slap, "there's no escape for you."

Four days later Martin Luther King sat on a park bench near the carousel in Central Park in Manhattan, talking under his breath to Harris Wofford. Wofford broke the news to King about his associates' connections with the Communist party, then waited for it to sink in. King was dumbfounded.

"I can't believe it's true," he said mournfully. "What proof is there? What evidence have you got that it's true?"

"I don't know if it's true, Martin. The FBI had their facts upside down when they checked me out. But listen to me: Hoover will leak these rumors to your enemies in Congress and the media as if they were facts."

King looked down. Wofford continued. "I believe that the best thing you can do, Martin, is break your ties with Levison and O'Dell."

King was in anguish. "For more than four years Stanley Levison has helped me, advised me. He negotiated the publishing deal for me, he even wrote the draft for the last chapter of the book. Harris, there's never been a hint of anything communistic about anything he's said or done. And he's always refused to let me pay him a penny for anything."

"What about O'Dell?"

"O'Dell is a Negro with integrity. He ran the SCLC fund-raising for two years. If he had any Communist connections, I'm sure he left them behind long ago."

"That's all they need to go on," warned Wofford.

"No. If the FBI has real proof of their present Communist connections, let them show it to me. Otherwise, I'm not going to break with my friends."

* * *

The phone call came late, but J. Edgar Hoover was up and ready for it.

"Mr. Hoover?"

"Yes, Junior."

"They've gone in. The phone taps are being installed in Levison's New York office right now."

"What about the bugs?"

". . . Sir, Kennedy's authorization only gave us the right to tap Levison's business phones."

"Since when has that stopped us?" Hoover growled. "Look, Junior, it's just another black-bag job. I want to know *everything* he does. King, too!"

The attorney general was in a good mood when he entered the inner office of the director of the FBI. He shook hands with Hoover, then Tolson. Exchanging pleasantries, he took a seat and asked Hoover what he had on his mind. Hoover glanced at Tolson and Tolson walked out, closing the door behind him. Hoover's tone became grave.

"I wish it was for a different reason that I've summoned you, one that was less dangerously explosive."

Kennedy was amused. "Well, you've got my attention, Edgar."

Hoover slumped in his chair, then straightened up. "Robert, as a result of the FBI surveillance of the gangsters and hoodlums you refer to as 'organized crime' that you've forced us to undertake . . . a matter of the utmost sensitivity has surfaced."

"Oh?" Kennedy was ready for more of Hoover's paranoia. He wasn't ready for what came next.

"While our agents had a gangster named Giancana under close observation several women were identified as frequent callers to Giancana's residence. All of the young women were carefully and quietly investigated."

"Go on."

"One of these women, the most frequent night visitor, was checked out in greater depth, she obviously being one of Giancana's favorites. We looked into her bank accounts, department store charges, travel charges . . . and her telephone records of course."

Enjoying the moment, Hoover paused, staring hard at the young and confident attorney general. Then he pounced.

"Bob . . . an examination of her outgoing calls revealed that she had placed a total of seventy calls to the president's office in the White House."

Suddenly the lightness and impatience went out of Bobby Kennedy. He turned red, his eyes narrowed, and he stared straight ahead. Hoover's attitude hardened.

"Her name is Judith Campbell. We questioned another of Giancana's girlfriends about her. The young woman stated that if we wanted to know more about Miss Campbell we should, quote, 'ask the President,' unquote."

Hoover handed Kennedy a file. In it were pictures of Judith Campbell. Kennedy looked up from the file a changed man. Bereft, depressed, he spoke in a voice both hard and flat.

"Thank you, Mr. Director."

Hoover stood, walked around his desk, and put his hand on Kennedy's shoulder. "I assure you, Mr. Attorney General, that I will treat this matter with the utmost discretion."

"Thank you, sir."

"Of course, if the president wishes to discuss this matter with me personally, I will give him everything we have that might be pertinent."

Bobby stood, shaken and defeated. "I'll pass that on. Thank you, Mr. Director, for bringing this to my attention."

When Bobby's back was turned, Hoover smiled triumphantly.

"Good day, Mr. Attorney General . . ."

Part II

CHAPTER 13

While John F. Kennedy, clad in a thick white terrycloth robe, scrutinized the FBI report on Judith Campbell, Robert Kennedy swam ten laps in the White House pool. Toweling off, the attorney general was still dripping when the president put down the file and picked up his orange juice.

"Okay Bobby," he said with a smile, "I'll put a stop to her phoning me."

"And you'll stop seeing her, too."

"Of course."

"Talk about stupid moves! It was just self-indulgence, Jack."

"You're the puritan, Bobby, not me."

"I wish you were."

Jack shrugged. "I don't."

Bobby picked up the file and pointed to the eight-by-ten of Judith Campbell in a skimpy bathing suit. "You think it's a coincidence she's one of Giancana's girls? You were set up, Jack!"

"There's no proof of that."

"It's obvious!"

The president sighed. "Look," he said, "I admit that I have an . . . excessive appetite, but . . ."

His brother interrupted. "Wait a minute. How did you meet Judith Campbell? Did you pick her up at the Inaugural Ball, or did you sweep her off her feet at one of the diplomatic receptions?"

"I was introduced to her."

"By whom?"

"Frank Sinatra."

For a moment the two brothers stared at each other. Bobby shook his head. "Look, Jack, stick with campaign workers and airline hostesses and movie stars, will you? I've got to have a free hand to go after Giancana and his friends."

JFK nodded his assent.

"Now," continued Bobby, "you're going to have lunch with Mr. Hoover tomorrow. Let him assure you that your secret is safe with him."

The president was annoyed. "Come on, Bobby, don't get carried away with all this Charlie Chan stuff. You're not my keeper. Not yet, anyway."

"I don't want to be your keeper," Bobby

replied tersely. "But with what Hoover has dug up, how long do you think it'll be before he finds out about the half-million dollars paid to your former fiancée back in the late forties?"

They held a look. Jack was the first to lower his eyes.

"Excellent lunch, Mr. President," said J. Edgar Hoover.

Hoover and Kennedy were in the Oval Office portico, the FBI director sitting in a straight-backed chair, the president in his favorite rocker. Hoover was clearly enjoying his renewed connection to the White House. They lit cigars.

"Thank you, Mr. Director," said Kennedy. "I have also ordered the dessert you favor. The cheesecake was delivered from your favorite restaurant."

Hoover beamed. "You shouldn't have gone to that trouble, Mr. President."

"My pleasure, Edgar."

"This is the way to deal with difficulties, sir," said Hoover. "Face to face."

The implication was not lost on JFK. "Edgar, I've often heard you are known to be a fair man."

Hoover smiled modestly.

". . . and that you are also a man who knows when to be discreet."

The director was fast to reply. "If I've learned

nothing else in all my years of government service, it is how to maintain 'prudent silence.'"

"An invaluable quality, Mr. Director."

Hoover smiled, then began cautiously. "Mr. President, the only other . . . suggestion I'd put forth . . . is that you reevaluate your friendship with Mr. Sinatra. He seems to mix his gangster friends, like Mr. Giancana, who stays in Mr. Sinatra's house occasionally, with his movie-star friends, like Marilyn Monroe . . . and your brother-in-law, Peter Lawford."

For a moment Kennedy gritted his teeth. "In the future I will, of course, avoid such potentially compromising situations."

Then he smiled mischievously, adding, "We all need to put more energy into curbing our appetites, wouldn't you say?"

J. Edgar Hoover, about to help himself to another slice of cheesecake, changed his mind.

"It's the undeniable truth." Marilyn Monroe was a little tipsy. Lounging at the bar in a huge party tent at the Rancho Mirage in California, the movie actress winked at the President. "I'm not making it up, Jack."

Jack smiled at Peter Lawford, then turned back to Marilyn. "You're putting me on."

"Okay," she said, "I'll prove it to you."

She reached for the telephone and almost fell off the bar stool. When Jack caught her she giggled and kissed him. He laughed and got the phone for her. She dialed and began talking with her hand over her mouth. Lawford got Kennedy's attention.

"Hey, I tried to get Frank on the phone, but when he gets his nose out of joint nobody gets through. Anyway, I left a message saying you wouldn't be staying at his house this trip."

"Or any other trip," said JFK flatly.

"Jack, Sinatra's spent a bundle on a heliport and a telecommunications center just for you. I don't know what to tell him now. He's going to be angry as hell."

Jack grinned. "Did somebody promise you life would be easy when you married into the Kennedy clan?"

Marilyn handed the telephone to Jack. "It's my masseur. He'll tell you about the muscles you claim don't exist."

Jack took the phone. "Hello?"

Marilyn winked at Peter Lawford. "I told you. Men don't have them. Just women."

She reached for her drink and missed. She got it on the second attempt, but Lawford took it away from her gently.

"I'll make you a fresh one," he said.

"No you won't! You'll just disappear. Then you'll come back later with cottage cheese and tell me I've got to eat that and then I can have a drink, right?"

Jack hung up. Lawford gave Marilyn a peck on the cheek and left with her glass.

"Hey! Come back with my drink!"

Jack pointed to the telephone. "That guy was your masseur?"

"Sure," she said, putting her arms around the president. "He knows my body better than anybody. Well, was I right or was I right?"

"I was wrong," said JFK, "and I apologize. He said that you've got those muscles and that they are highly developed."

She giggled. "You may kiss my hand."

He kissed it.

"And then you can tell me why you feel the need to fool around with these other movie actresses who are less talented and less beautiful than me."

Lawford reappeared at that moment with a dish of fruit and cottage cheese. Marilyn slapped it out of his hand, causing people to turn and stare at the celebrity threesome.

"Well," said Marilyn breathlessly, "I'm waiting for an answer, Mr. President."

John Fitzgerald Kennedy was at a loss for words.

Angie Novello's voice came over Robert Kennedy's intercom. "Sorry to interrupt, sir, but Mr. Houston and Mr. Edwards of the CIA are here."

Kennedy dismissed the three aides who were working with him in his Justice Department office and told his secretary to admit the CIA men. Houston and Edwards, well-dressed and immaculately groomed, appeared a moment later. They closed the door and stood before Bobby's desk holding their hands behind them.

The attorney general's tone was brusque. "Last night," he began, rising from his chair, "one of your people asked me to drop a case we are currently prosecuting in Las Vegas against Robert Maheu for an illegal wiretap." Kennedy paused to let the information sink in, then continued.

"When I asked why I should drop the case I was told that the wiretap was placed there by the Central Intelligence Agency as a 'favor to someone.'"

The CIA men said nothing.

"When I asked to know the name of this important 'someone,' I was told it was Sam Giancana. This morning I received a confidential memo from J. Edgar Hoover which contains portions of a wiretapped conversation between Giancana and a friend of his in which he states, 'Fidel Castro is to be done away with shortly.'"

Kennedy jabbed a finger at Houston and Edwards. "What the hell is going on?" he demanded.

Houston was the first to speak. "It's part of Operation Mongoose, Mr. Attorney General," he said lamely.

Bobby was incredulous. "Do you mean that the CIA has made a deal with a Mafia rat like Giancana to get Castro? This is ridiculous! I've got thirty men working around the clock to get Giancana convicted of something, anything, and you are employing him to do highly sensitive, top-secret CIA work?"

Edwards replied. "Mr. Attorney General, it was decided that the most effective way to destroy Castro's regime was to have it done by anti-Castro Cuban gangsters."

"Why?"

"Because they're the most motivated, sir. But we can't help it if that includes some Cubans who had strong links with American gambling interests that were thrown out of Cuba when Castro took over."

"I never authorized Operation Mongoose to get in bed with the Mafia!"

"It all went through our normal channels," said Houston. "We started with Maheu, who led us to Giancana, who made the deal with the underground Cuban gangsters."

Furious, Bobby raised his voice. "What do you mean 'it went through normal channels'? Does that mean that Dulles approved of this insanity?"

"We presumed so . . ."

"You presumed? And Richard Helms, too?"

"Yes," replied Edwards. "The same way that we presumed that this project was cleared with the president."

Bobby was stopped cold in his tracks.

One hour later the president and the attorney general took a slow walk together through the

White House Rose Garden. John F. Kennedy listened to his brother's information without comment. When the attorney general had finished the president shook his head.

"Bobby, they never told me they were going to recruit Maheu and Giancana."

"You've got to put a muzzle on John McCone and Richard Helms," said Robert Kennedy.

"I will. But you've got to remember that as the director and deputy director of the CIA, McCone and Helms have grown accustomed to running their own little empire."

"I know that . . ."

"Let me finish. This Castro thing was hatched when Eisenhower was president. So was the Bay of Pigs invasion. I inherited them, Bobby. Not that that relieves me of any of the responsibility."

"We're both responsible, Jack. But it's not too late."

"What do you want me to do?"

"Cut Giancana loose. Then I can prosecute him without it blowing up in all our faces."

"Okay, Bobby, I'll do it."

Bobby shrugged. JFK patted his back. "Dad was right," he said with a smile. "You're the only one I can trust."

Bobby Kennedy was stretched out on a couch in his office, reading a thick government report, when Harris Wofford entered and dropped into a chair beside the attorney general. Kennedy pointed to an untouched birthday cake thick with candles.

"You missed the party, Harris," he said.

Wofford grinned. "What kind of a party was it? Nobody ate the cake."

"It was a celebration of J. Edgar Hoover's thrity-eighth year as director of the FBI."

"What happened?"

"Well, the guest of honor didn't show up. He was having a snit. Have a piece of cake."

Wofford passed up the cake. "What was Hoover mad about?"

"Who knows?"

Wofford was annoyed. "Come on, Bobby," he said. "Why are you trying to put a good face on it? Hoover hates your guts. He couldn't even bring himself to come here and be cordial."

"I know," Bobby admitted. Then he changed the subject. "So Harris, are you making your constituents happy?"

"I've told the president that I'm leaving the White House to go to work for the Peace Corps in Africa."

Alarmed, Bobby sat up. "Wait a minute, Harris. We need you as a buffer with the Negro leaders, Martin Luther King in particular. You know that."

"I don't think there should be a 'buffer' between the Negro people and the administration, Bobby. They don't need an interpreter."

J. Edgar Hoover (Jack Warden) with his only friend and confidant, Clyde Tolson (Marc Strange), in the background.

A triumphant John Kennedy (Robert Pine) is led through crowds of supporters on his way to accept the Democratic party's nomination for the presidency.

Martin Luther King, Jr., (Leland Gantt) and his wife Coretta (Djanet Sears) are approached by the media following his release from prison as arranged by Robert Kennedy.

One of a seemingly endless series of confrontations between FBI Director J. Edgar Hoover and the man who was, in theory, his superior, Attorney General Robert Kennedy (Nicholas Campbell).

The young Attorney General, Robert Kennedy, toils into the wee hours in his Justice Department office.

During the historic civil rights demonstration, Freedom Riders are attacked by hostile crowds.

Family patriarch Joseph Kennedy, Sr., (Barry Morse) is confronted by his two sons over alleged campaign contributions from unsavory characters.

The Reverend Martin Luther King, Jr., addresses hundreds of thousands of people during the march on Washington.

Robert Kennedy confronts his brother John with J. Edgar Hoover's confidential file on the president's "indiscretions" involving a woman named Judith Campbell.

Marilyn Monroe (Heather Thomas) sings "Happy Birthday, Mr. President" at Madison Square Garden.

Robert Kennedy on his "mission" to California to break off the liaison between Marilyn Monroe and his brother, the president.

An irate J. Edgar Hoover reacts viciously to a report that there is no evidence to support his belief that the American civil rights movement has been infiltrated by Communists.

An emotionally overwrought Robert Kennedy attempts to bar newly sworn in President Lyndon Johnson (Richard Anderson) from entering the Oval Office, in the wake of the tragic assassination of John F. Kennedy.

The remaining members of the first family prepare for the funeral of their beloved husband and father: Caroline (Carol Lynch), Jackie (Jennifer Dale), and John Kennedy, Jr., (Alex Richardson).

J. Edgar Hoover poses for a picture alongside President Lyndon Johnson on the occasion of the signing of the historic civil rights bill.

"That's not what I meant."

"Perhaps not. But that's the way it's turned out. I think it's vital that you and the president deal directly with King and the other Negro leaders. That is the only way you have a chance to understand their true feelings, their reality."

Bobby sighed. "First Seigenthaler leaves to run the *Nashville Tennessean,* and now you're off to Africa. Is the ship sinking, Harris? Is that why you two guys jumped off?"

Wofford smiled sadly. "The ship isn't sinking, Bobby. I don't think that. No one does. I'm going to Africa, but I'll be back."

"I'm very sad that you're going, Harris. You'll keep in touch?"

The two men rose and shook hands. As Wofford left the office, Mavis Winters, a black cleaning lady in her fifties, entered with a broom and dustpan. Kennedy pointed to the uneaten cake.

"Can I interest you in some chocolate cake, Mavis?"

"No, thank you kindly, Mr. Kennedy," she replied. "I'd only eat it and put on pounds. But you've got a house full of children, Mr. Kennedy. I'm sure they'd make it disappear in no time."

"You're right," Bobby replied. "And if my kids knew I almost gave it away I'd be a goner."

"I'm sure you would, sir."

Kennedy, tired and melancholy, put on his overcoat.

"Mavis, I'm putting you on the payroll as one of my advisors!"

Marilyn Monroe was late, very late. Somewhat drunk and wearing a skintight, backless dress, she allowed two security guards to help her through the crowded backstage area of Madison Square Garden. Peter Lawford took her arm.

"Do you know how late you are, Marilyn? Do you know how many times I've told them you're on your way?"

"Don't talk to me, Peter," she pleaded. "I'll forget my lines."

Marilyn appeared onstage beneath a huge banner reading Happy Birthday Mr. President. Lawford waited for the applause to die out, then took the microphone.

"Ladies and gentlemen, Mr. President, in the history of show business perhaps there has been no one female who has meant so much, who has done more . . . Mr. President . . . Marilyn Monroe!"

Bobby, Ethel, and Jack sat together in the presidential box. Jackie's seat was empty. They looked up at Marilyn as she stood nervously before the microphone and began to sing.

She sang "Happy Birthday" in the voice of a ten-year-old. No one cared. They loved her.

CHAPTER 14

The driver of the limousine wore a cheap suit, had a two-day growth of beard, and chewed on a cigar stub. As he scanned the racing form, his fingers toyed with the volume control of the battery-powered tape recorder on the seat beside him. He was checking the odds on the fourth race at Del Mar when the attorney general's voice came over his earpiece.

". . . They're talking about making a movie of the book I wrote," Bobby said.

The limo driver adjusted the earpiece and the volume.

". . . Yeah, some friend," replied Peter Lawford. "The part's perfect for me, but they're talking to Paul Newman."

Then Marilyn Monroe interrupted. "Where

are you going with my drink, Peter-Peter Pumpkin Eater?''

Less than a mile away, Marilyn, Bobby and Lawford were sitting around a white wrought-iron table on Lawford's patio. To insure privacy, the servants had been given the day off, and Lawford was mixing the drinks. He held Marilyn's half-empty glass in his hand.

"I was just going to freshen it for you, sweetheart."

"Why do I trust you?" she breathed.

When Lawford had gone, Bobby touched Marilyn's hand.

"Marilyn, there is something I have to talk to you about," he said.

A shadow crossed Marilyn's face. "I hope you're not bringing me a 'Dear John' letter from Jack." Her mouth trembled. "You're not, are you?"

"Let's go for a walk on the beach."

The limo driver turned up the volume. The "subjects" were moving around again. He could still hear Marilyn.

"Peter? Where's my drink?"

Then Bobby, faintly. "Just for a few minutes, Marilyn. Come on."

Then the voices turned into mumbles, and finally silence. The driver turned off the tape recorder and went back to the racing form.

Angie Novello waited for Bobby to look up

from the papers on his desk at the Justice Department. When he did she spoke quietly.

"Miss Monroe called again."

"How did she sound?"

"The same," said his secretary, looking away. "She said she'd call again in an hour."

Bobby shook his head and checked his desk calendar.

"I'll be back in California on Friday. Tell her I'll call her then."

Angie nodded and walked out.

Bill Sullivan entered J. Edgar Hoover's office, greeted the director, and remained standing.

"I thought you'd want to know, Mr. Hoover. Marilyn Monroe has been phoning the attorney general."

Hoover smiled, rubbing his hands. "Fine, fine. I want to know everything, Bill. When he meets with her, where, how long, *everything*, understand?"

"Yessir, Mr. Hoover."

Bobby scanned the pages before him. They were a neatly typed transcript of a wiretapped conversation between Stanley Levison and Martin Luther King. He read aloud to Courtney Evans:

Levison: O'Dell had ties with the Communist party. That was a few years ago, but it's a fact, Martin.

King: That doesn't pose a problem for me.

Levison: What do you mean?

King: No matter what a man was, if he can stand up now and say he was not connected, then as far as I'm concerned he can work for me.

Bobby put down the file and looked at Evans. Evans spoke.

"Jack O'Dell was elected to the Communist party's national committee in December, 1959, under the pseudonym 'Cornelius Jones.'"

"I got that," said Bobby. "And Levison was the one who got O'Dell the job with the SCLC in the first place."

Evans knitted his brow. "Mr. Hoover feels strongly that this is a clear example of Levison spinning his Communist web around King and the civil rights movement."

Bobby shook his head. "Come on, Courtney . . . Next you'll be telling me Khrushchev runs the Civil Rights Movement."

Clyde Tolson handed Hoover a fresh bag of popcorn and sat beside him on the couch. Filling the TV screen before them was the well-known image of Marilyn Monroe in a scene from *The Seven Year Itch;* she was standing over a sidewalk grating while an air blast blew up her skirt. The announcer's voice was somber.

. . . And on the way she learned how to act. She married and divorced Joe DiMaggio and playwright Arthur Miller. She caroused with such as Yves Montand, Frank Sinatra, Marlon Brando and Peter Lawford . . .

Hoover nudged Tolson. They both nodded.

. . . Death, caused by an apparently accidental overdose of barbiturates, according to the Los Angeles County Coroner, brings to an end the life of another Hollywood legend, the sex symbol of her generation, the star who wanted the world to take her seriously.

"How old was she?" Tolson asked.
"Thirty-six."
Tolson shook his head. Hoover turned off the set and grabbed another fistful of popcorn.
"When the time come we'll expose the facts."

The radio blared in the attorney general's office.

. . . Eighteen months ago James Meredith, an Air Force veteran, applied for admission to the University of Mississippi, an institution of higher learning where Negroes have never been allowed to attend. The NAACP, with the support of the attorney general, Robert Kennedy and the local field secretary Medger Evers, spearheads the challenge against Mississippi's governor, Ross Barnett, in a battle that could suddenly change from one of words and court orders to one of racial violence.

It was Tuesday, September 25, 1962, at 12:20 P.M., and Bobby Kennedy was on the phone to Governor Barnett.

". . . Governor Barnett, you are still a part of the United States," Kennedy said matter-of-factly.

The governor was hesitant. "Well, we have been a part of the United States, but now I don't know whether we are or not."

"Are you getting out of the Union?"

Barnett could not conceal his anger and frustration. "Does it have to be over one little boy who's backed by the NAACP, which is a Communist front?"

"I don't think it is, Governor."

"Down here we *know* it is," snapped Barnett. "We know pretty well what's going on. I think he's being paid by some left-wing organization to do all this. He has no income, but he's riding around here in two great big Cadillacs. Who's giving him all this money?"

"Governor," said Bobby wearily, "those great big Cadillacs are government cars. Meredith has no money."

"You must appreciate my position, Mr. Kennedy. I have said that there will be no integration at Ole Miss so often that I cannot back down without the direst consequences."

Five days later, on September 30, Bobby placed another call to Barnett. Kennedy's tone, along with recent events, had changed.

"Governor," he said flatly, "we will not postpone Mr. Meredith's admission any longer."

There was a pause on the other end of the line, then:

"Mr. Attorney General, I cannot have my troopers step aside unless the U.S. marshals draw their pistols."

"Governor . . . we will not have our marshals draw their guns. That would be a silly and dangerous farce."

"You must confront me with troops!"

Bobby played a trump card. "The president is going on television tonight, and he will have to explain that he's called up the Mississippi National Guard because you have broken an agreement with him to allow Mr. Meredith to register yesterday."

"Oh no!" yelped the governor. "He can't do that!"

"I'm afraid, Governor Barnett, that he will . . . unless you promise to preserve law and order with your own peace officers, so that Mr. Meredith can register."

There was a pause.

"All right," replied the governor. "We will recognize the authority of the federal marshals, and our highway patrolmen will lend every assistance."

Kennedy allowed a little warmth to enter his voice.

"Governor, we have no objection to your saying you are yielding to an overwhelming force, or that you will continue to fight this in the courts . . . *as long as you maintain order.*"

Governor Barnett said he understood, and hung up.

That same night, in the Oval Office, President Kennedy addressed the nation on television. He appeared tired but determined:

> . . . A series of federal courts, all the way to the Supreme Court, repeatedly ordered Mr. Meredith's admission to the university. When those orders were defied, the United States Court of Appeals made clear the fact that the enforcement of its order had become an obligation of the United States government. It was for this reason that I federalized the Mississippi National Guard.

Kennedy allowed a moment to pass, then continued.

> Neither Mississippi nor any other southern state deserves to be charged with all the accumulated wrongs of the past one hundred years of race relations. However, the most effective means of upholding the law is not the state policemen, or the marshals, or the national guard. It is you, the citizens of Mississippi.
>
> Let us preserve both the law and the peace, and stand united as one people in our pledge to man's freedom.

The president stared hard at the TV camera, then nodded.

"Thank you and good night."

The moment the TV floor manager signaled that the president was off the air, the door opened and the attorney general and Burke Marshall rushed in. While the TV crew cleared the office of their gear, the three men huddled.

Bobby whispered in the president's ear. "It's escalating, Jack! Just as you were going on the air Katzenbach phoned me. He says the U.S. marshals were forced to fire tear gas in self-defense, to control the mob. But they also accidentally gassed a number of the state troopers."

Burke Marshall was agitated. "It gets worse, sir. The state troopers had no gas masks, so they had to withdraw. A marshal's been shot. Katzenback wants to know if the marshals can use their pistols."

John Kennedy waved a finger. "Absolutely not. There will be no firearms unless Meredith is in danger. Is that clear? Bobby, call Katzenbach and tell him."

Bobby was already dialing. "Nick? You there? Okay. The president says the marshals cannot use their pistols unless Meredith is in danger. What's the situation now?"

On the other end of the line, sitting at a makeshift command post in the Lyceum hallway of Ole Miss, Nicholas Katzenbach spoke hoarsely into the phone.

"It's not good, Bobby. But I still want to try to settle this without calling in the army. Ask the president to put the screws to Governor Barnett again."

"Nick, if things get rough, don't worry about yourself. The president needs a moral issue," Bobby said ironically.

Katzenbach hung up in time to hear the big, square-jawed Jim McShane, chief U.S. marshal, bark instructions to several of his men, who were dressed in business suits and white helmets. Gas masks pushed up on their heads, shoulder holsters peeking from under open jackets, the men were combat ready and waiting to be unleashed. In the middle of McShane's speech, Katzenbach interrupted.

"No guns!" he shouted. "Orders from the president."

Several of the men lowered themselves to the floor, where they sat nursing injuries from bricks and stones. A few frightened students tried to calm a bruised and confused professor, who kept repeating, "Why? Why?"

In the Oval Office, the president had Governor Barnett on the line. While Kennedy listened he shot glances at his brother and scribbled notes.

"Mr. President," drawled the governor, "I have indeed ordered the state troopers back to the campus. But there are not enough of them, I am afraid, to restore order. You *must* remove Meredith from here."

"Now wait a minute, governor," snapped JFK. "First, you restore order. Then we'll talk about Meredith."

Bobby Kennedy, on the phone to Katzenbach, shouted across the room, "Three marshals have been shot! Shotguns! They're running low on tear gas! Nick says the situation is out of hand. He wants the army. He says the mob is growing, not just local students, either. The rednecks are coming in with their shotguns all the way from Georgia."

JFK picked up a special telephone and spoke slowly and clearly. "Get the army troops onto the campus. *Now*."

Two hours later, at two-thirty in the morning, an exhausted Katzenbach limped down the Lyceum hallway to the phone. Sitting along both sides of the hall, the injured and wounded waited for medical attention. Outside, occasional rifle shots could still be heard. Three soldiers in combat gear were smoking cigarettes and looking furtively through a broken window. Katzenbach picked up the phone and dialed Bobby Kennedy in Washington.

"It's all over. The regulars just routed the mob. They're mopping up and the marshals are making arrests. It's been bloody, Bobby . . ."

The attorney general put down the phone. In the Oval Office, only he, the president, and Burke Marshall remained. Red-eyed, Bobby repeated Katzenbach's figures.

"Of the four hundred and twenty-six marshals, one hundred and sixty have been injured. Twenty-eight of them were shot."

The president held his face in his hands. Then he looked up. "Have we started the Second Civil War?" he asked.

"No," said Bobby. "I think we're preventing it. We're preserving the Union."

"What do we do now?" Burke Marshal queried.

Bobby permitted himself a smile. "Well, I guess we register Mr. Meredith at 8 A.M."

At 9 A.M. the next morning Angie Novello peeked in the attorney general's office and saw RFK fast asleep on the couch. She returned to her office, put her bag and coffee container on the desk, and turned on the morning news.

. . . The night of violence resulted in two murders, twenty-eight marshals shot, and over one hundred and sixty people injured. It is a victory with tragic overtones for the Justice Department and its young attorney general, Robert Kennedy. After almost two years of struggle, a Negro air force veteran, James Meredith, is a student at the University of Mississippi, the first Negro ever to be admitted . . .

Angie sighed. In the years she had been working for him she had never been prouder of Bobby Kennedy.

CHAPTER 15

J. Edgar Hoover swatted at a fly and missed. He looked up as Helen Gandy ushered in Courtney Evans, who wore a worried look.

"What now?" Hoover demanded.

"Sir, the attorney general wants to know when the FBI will open a field office in Mississippi."

Irate, Hoover fired back at him, "You tell him that *nobody* tells me where to open an FBI office!"

"I will, Mr. Hoover." Evans remained standing, but looked wistfully at the door.

"And tell the little sonofabitch he's got no call to grouse. He's been getting information from our agents down there quicker than I have."

"Yessir."

". . . all this fuss over getting one Negra into school. All right, Evans, get on with it."

As Courtney Evans hurried out he nearly collided with Sullivan and Tolson, who were on their way in. Hoover nodded to them and pushed a button on his intercom.

"Miss Gandy, will you send Sam in here with his flyswatter?" Then, in the same breath, he told his chief aides to be seated.

Clyde Tolson cleared his throat. "Mr. Hoover, the attorney general has decided to take a tour of our FBI offices across the country. New York, Chicago, St. Louis, our biggest bureaus . . ."

"God damn him!" Hoover barked. "How *dare* he?" Suddenly the director's mood swung. "He has, huh? Okay, when is he going to Chicago?"

Sullivan spoke up. "Next week, sir. I think he leaves on Wednesday."

Breathless, Sam Noisette arrived carrying a flyswatter. Hoover held up his hand for silence and pointed to a spot on the paneled wall. "Sam, there it is . . ."

Noisette saw the fly and went after it.

"Bill," said Hoover, "I think this is an opportunity, an excellent opportunity for us to protect ourselves."

"Sir?"

"Look here. Have Evans make sure the attorney general visits our Chicago office."

"Yes sir."

"You're excused, Billy."

Sullivan left.

Sam Noisette raised the flyswatter, tracking it

across the office. The fly settled on Hoover's arm.

"There it is, Sam!"

Sam was hesitant.

"Well, kill it!"

"But it's on your arm, sir."

"I don't give a damn, kill it!"

Sam struck, Hoover winced, and the fly fell to the floor. Sam picked it up and left.

"Junior, listen carefully. You will arrange for Chicago to have an interesting collection of tapes for the attorney general to hear. Some of the tapes will be legal telephone bugs . . ."

"And some will be surveillance bugs," said Tolson.

"He won't know the difference."

"Of course not."

"Has contact been made with Martin Luther King about his statement in the *New York Times?*"

"Dexter called him," Tolson said. "Harding in Atlanta called him. King has not returned either of their calls."

"What? We can't let King get away with telling lies about the bureau!"

"No sir."

"All right, Junior. I want you to find proof that King's embezzling SCLC money for his high living."

"Yessir."

"You're excused."

* * *

Ten days later, Bobby Kennedy, on a guided tour of the Chicago FBI field office, joined a group of agents in a small conference room where a collection of tapes were played for him. He listened carefully to the recorded conversations of various mobsters and their underlings. When the last tape had been played he rose.

"Very interesting," he said.

"We'd appreciate any comments you may have, Mr. Attorney General."

"Comments? What can I say? It's apparent that you're collecting information that I hope will lead to many convictions."

"Thank you, sir, and thanks for dropping by."

When Kennedy left the agents exchanged a knowing look.

The trap was set.

On the night of May 9, 1963, the attorney general sat alone in his office, watching a recap of the April 25 riots in Birmingham. The narrator spoke without emotion.

> . . . Thousands of Birmingham Negro high school students marched down the streets in a nonviolent demonstration and were assaulted with high pressure fire hoses and police dogs on orders from Police Chief Bull Connor.

Bobby grabbed a telephone.

"Burke? No, I'm watching it right now. Hold a second."

. . . When it was over almost twenty-five-hundred people were arrested, many of them children. No figures are available on how many were injured . . .

"Burke? I'm holding on the other line for Joe Rauh. You know, the attorney for the United Auto Workers. He's going to confirm the bail money for the Birmingham demonstrators."

At that moment the phone in Bobby's other hand came alive. He held it to his ear.

"Yes, this is the attorney general. Please put Mr. Rauh on. Yes. Joe! Have you worked it out? You have? That's great! Tell me, how many arms did you have to twist? Four arms for $160,000 in bail money? That's not bad! Okay, have your bank wire confirmation to Birmingham. Thanks, Joe, I owe you one . . ."

As RFK hung up Angie Novello entered.

"Excuse me, sir, but Ed Guthman wants to know if you want to make a statement on Hoffa's indictment for jury tampering."

"No," said Bobby, "not until there's a conviction." As his secretary left, Mavis Winters entered with her mop, broom, and dustpan. Bobby nodded to her and got back on the phone.

"Burke? Yes, it's done. Yes, the UAW and three other unions. No, I still don't think they should have put their children in danger like that. Okay, later, Burke."

From the other side of the room the office

maid muttered, "Those children have been in danger from the day they were born."

Bobby heard. "Were you speaking to me, Mavis?" he inquired politely.

"Yes sir."

"Please go on."

"Sir, it don't make no difference," said the tired-looking black cleaning woman. "Every day is a trial if you're colored. Better those children learn early."

She went on cleaning the office.

The thin, dark figure waited patiently in the corridor outside J. Edgar Hoover's office. At 6 P.M., when the director of the FBI finally emerged, alone and carrying a battered briefcase, the thin man approached him.

"Mr. Hoover," he said, "you probably don't remember me, but my name is Denton."

"Of course I remember you," snapped Hoover. "You're the agent I fired yesterday for having an extramarital affair!"

"That's what I wanted to talk to you about, Mr. Hoover."

Hoover stood back, looked the ex-agent over from head to toe, and said, "There is nothing to talk about. You chose to violate the code I demand all agents live by and . . ."

"But Mr. Hoover, the circumstances were such that . . ."

Hoover, who could not stand being interrupted, raised his voice.

"You thought I might reconsider? That I might compromise my standards for the bureau?"

"Sir," said Denton, "you have no right to fire me because of anything I do in my personal life that has no effect on my performance with the bureau."

"No right?" sputtered the director. "I have every right! You have a *disease*, Mr. Denton! It's running rampant in this country! You and Kennedy and King and many others crawl from bed to bed and from woman to woman like perverse sexual beasts! Your morals are contemptible!"

"Mr. Hoover, please . . ."

"And what about the women? What about your wives, who should be revered instead of being betrayed by your loathsome corruption of your marriage vows? And the shame for your children? *I* have no right? Why, you and the rest of your kind are lucky! If I had my way, the punishment for your despicable behavior would be a lot worse, believe me!"

Hoover moved past Denton and into the elevator, scowling at him until the doors closed.

On Sunday, May 24, 1963, a group of prominent black Americans met with Bobby Kennedy and Burke Marshall in Joseph Kennedy's luxurious New York apartment. Among the guests were Harry Belafonte, Lena Horne, Clarence Jones, James Baldwin, and Jerome Smith. When Bobby had thanked the group for coming, he said the reason for the meeting was to discuss civil rights problems and possible solutions. He said he was interested in anything they had to say. Lena Horne began.

"Why don't you send in the army? There must be a million men who could be doing something useful."

Bobby faced her. "Calling in the army would mean declaring martial law. And curfews. And no demonstrations. And empty streets and closed businesses. Everybody loses that way. Our approach is to get whites and Negroes together, talking, negotiating, enforcing court orders. It takes time. We're not going to change segregation overnight."

Harry Belafonte spoke up. "Bobby, first of all it's crazy to think we can spend a few hours together and actually convey to you all the things in this country that need fixing as far as we're concerned."

"Well," asked Bobby, "how about just a few, then? We can meet again, as long as it takes. We're drafting new civil rights legislation right now, and I'd like your input. I'd like it very much. How about you, James?"

James Baldwin sat on the arm of a couch. "I'm in, we all are. We'll try to be honest, to say what we feel. It won't help to censor one another."

"We're just not sure how much of the truth you can take," said Clarence Jones.

Lena Horne smiled. "You see, the problem is

that you haven't had any of the experiences that we've had all our lives."

Bobby lifted his hands. "I asked for this meeting so that maybe we can begin to understand. I've known about racial prejudice all my life. My brother is the grandson of an Irish immigrant, and today he's the president of the United States. So you should understand that this is possible: that in the next fifty years or so a Negro can be president."

An awkward, embarrassed silence followed, broken at last by James Baldwin.

"Bobby, my family has been in this country for generations. I really don't think we're any closer to the presidency."

Bobby ignored the remark. "I think that the record my brother and I have made concerning the enforcement of civil rights laws and the bills that we will soon put before Congress speak for themselves."

"I don't give a rat's ass about you or your brother."

Everyone looked at Jerome Smith. Smith was a young civil rights worker who began as a Gandhian pacifist, became a Freedom Rider and a CORE field worker. According to the CORE historians Smith had probably spent more time in jail and been beaten more often than any other member of the organization. At the time, he was in New York for medical treatment for his injuries, and he was angry.

Harry Belafonte tried to shift focus. "Bob, you and your brother have a lot of credit banked with the Negro people. The question is, when are you going to start using that credit?"

"Why are you leaning on us this way?" Bobby was genuinely confused. "There hasn't been another administration in history that's done what we have for civil rights."

"Bullcrap!" shouted Jerome Smith. "In wartime, when you need my muscle, when you need my blood, I'm an American citizen. But in the meantime I'm garbage!"

Bobby reddened. "Would you take up arms in defense of America?"

"Hell no! Never!"

"Even if the Russians attacked?"

"You shouldn't be worried about the Russians!" Smith fired back. "All your talk about our foreign enemies . . . the real enemies, the real dangers, are *inside*, right here in America!"

"Which dangers?" Bobby asked.

Smith stuttered when he was angry, but he tried to control it. "Where've you been, man?" he asked, pointing a finger at Kennedy. "The dangers are racism, unemployment, violence, lousy schools! If you're white, all right—if you're black, step back!"

"Look here, Mr. Smith," said Bobby evenly, "we were the first administration ever to enforce the Constitution in the southern states."

It was Clarence Jones' turn to be irate. "Is that why Dr. King and Dr. Shuttlesworth and forty-five hundred Negroes filled the jails of Birmingham, with twenty thousand more waiting to get in? Is that why Bull Connor turned on the fire hoses?"

"You didn't do doodle-de-dick!" shouted Smith. "We were American citizens taking a bus ride and we got the crap beat out of us! We . . ."

Burke Marshall tried to defuse the situation.

"We'll never get anywhere," he said, "if we keep on making this personal."

"It is personal!" blurted Clarence Jones.

Lena Horne smiled at Jerome Smith. "Let the man talk," she said.

Smith made a fist. "It just makes me sick." He stared hard at Bobby Kennedy. "It's like I could vomit, just being in the same room with you."

"Why is that?" asked the attorney general.

"Because you sit in your big clean Washington office with a full belly, and you have no idea what it means to be born in this country with a different color skin!"

The gathering was taken aback at the intensity of Smith's response. They let him speak his fill, knowing that in his own way he was speaking for all of them, for all the blacks in America.

"Whose attorney general are you?" Smith demanded. "You're not *my* attorney general! You're just another white man shuckin' and jivin' me!"

Smith pulled up the sleeves of his shirt and showed Kennedy the vicious scars.

"Where was my attorney general when they did this to me?"

He bent forward so that Bobby could see the scars on his scalp.

"How about this? Where were you when they were doing this to me?"

Smith stood, ripped off his shirt and turned his back to Bobby, revealing the numerous chain scars. He fell to his knees weeping.

"Where was my attorney general when they were doing this? Did you Kennedy brothers hear me when I screamed? Can you hear us now?"

Robert Kennedy looked about the silent room and nodded solemnly. The awareness of the gulf that separated him from the others who were gathered there was just beginning to penetrate his consciousness.

"Let me begin again . . ."

CHAPTER 16

"Let's start pressing these nigras and nigra lovers, Junior." J. Edgar Hoover looked up from his cheesecake and grinned. "Mail covers, agent visits to business associates, neighbors, friends. We'll send leaks to our favorite columnists—the works. Let's make them squirm, Clyde."

"Yes sir." Clyde Tolson's look was grim.

"You all right, Clyde?"

"Well, sir, I've been seeing the doctors . . ."

"And?"

"Looks like they want to sew up the old pump."

Hoover moved to Tolson's side. "Oh God, Clyde, no . . ."

Jack and Bobby Kennedy stared at the portable television in disbelief. Alone together in the

143

Oval Office, they watched Alabama's Governor George Wallace rant and rave about upholding the values of the Old South, declaring that no Negro would ever be allowed to enter the University of Alabama.

"Is it true that you once posed for a picture with your arm around that man?" asked Bobby.

"Untrue," said his brother.

"It could have been a long time ago."

"Impossible."

"Why are you so sure?"

"Because I've never posed for a picture with my arm around anyone," said John Fitzgerald Kennedy.

Bobby's eyes shone with admiration. The brothers returned their attention to the TV.

"Looks like a rerun of Ole Miss," said JFK.

"Wallace will have us doing the same dance we did with Governor Barnett until we allow him to save face. That means calling out the army or the guard," said RFK.

"Well, keep talking to him for a few days. See if we can avoid calling in the troops."

"Jack," said Bobby thoughtfully, "we can't afford to turn this issue into a political football. It's a moral issue."

"I agree."

"Especially after what happened in Birmingham. Thousands of Negro children dragged off to jail for daring to stage a peaceful protest."

"I haven't forgotten."

"Jack, the country is polarizing. We can't

afford to let that happen. You've got to go to the people and speak to the moral issue."

"All right," said the president. "I will."

Three nights later, on Wednesday, June 11, 1963, JFK addressed the nation from the Oval Office. Behind him a navy-blue velour cloth was draped over a sheet of plywood. On it was mounted the presidential seal.

> Good evening, my fellow citizens. This afternoon, following a series of threats and defiant statements, the presence of Alabama national guardsmen was required on the campus of the University of Alabama to carry out the final and unequivocal order of the United States District Court of the Northern District of Alabama. That order called for the admission of two clearly qualified young Alabama residents who happened to have been born Negro.

Watching the President from nearby was Bobby Kennedy. He looked away as Burke Marshall entered the Oval Office and hurried over to him. While the two men whispered, the president continued his address.

> We are confronted by a *moral* issue. It is as old as the Scriptures and as clear as the American Constitution. The heart of the question is whether all Americans are to be afforded equal rights and equal opportunities, whether we are going to treat our fellow

Americans as we want to be treated. When
Americans are sent to Vietnam or West Berlin
we do not ask for whites only . . .

Martin and Coretta King sat in their living
room watching the president's address. Their
three eldest children—Yolanda, age seven; Martin III, five; and Dexter, two—seemed as interested in the speech as their parents. The
president was warming to his subject.

> We preach freedom around the world and
> we mean it. But are we to say to the world, and
> to each other, that this is the land of the free
> *except* for the Negroes? That we have no class
> or caste system, no ghettos, no master race,
> except with respect to Negroes?

"They've come a long way," said Martin Luther King.

"You've been pushing for this now for more
than eight years, Martin," said Coretta. "I'm so
proud of you."

"What a day," said King. "Governor Wallace
stepped aside. The doors to the University of
Alabama are now open. And now John Kennedy
has galvanized the nation."

Coretta hugged her husband. "You're home at
last, dear. Thank God Almighty, you're home at
last."

At the White House, Burke Marshall, Bobby
Kennedy, and Courtney Evans huddled in Mrs.
Lincoln's office outside the Oval Office. They

spoke in whispers, their eyes riveted to the portable TV screen.

"Mr. Hoover asked me to interrupt whatever you were doing, sir," said Evans.

"Quick! What is it?" Bobby asked.

"Sir, a white man just shot and killed the NAACP field secretary in Mississippi, Medgar Evers. It happened on the steps of his home in Jackson."

Bobby's face saddened. Marshall shook his head. On television the president continued;

. . . One hundred years have passed since President Lincoln freed the slaves. Yet their grandsons are not fully free. Now the time has come for this nation to fulfill its promises. Next week I shall ask the Congress of the United States to act, to make a commitment it has not made in this century, to the proposition that race has no place in American life or law. But legislation, I repeat, cannot solve this problem alone. It must be solved in the homes of all Americans in every community across our country . . .

Without breaking his concentration, Bobby picked up a telephone. "Operator, this is the attorney general. Get me Charles Evers, please. He's probably at the home of Medgar Evers in Jackson, Mississippi. Thanks, I'll hold . . ."

John F. Kennedy concluded his address;

We have a right to expect that the Negro

community will be responsible, will uphold the law. But they have a right to expect that the law will be fair, that the Constitution will be color-blind. This is a matter which concerns this country and what it stands for, and in meeting it I ask for the support of all our citizens. Thank you very much.

Courtney Evans touched Bobby's arm. "I'm sorry, Mr. Kennedy," he said. "Mr. Hoover wants to know if there is anything you want him to do regarding this unfortunate occurrence, other than to conduct a full investigation, of course."

To this Robert Kennedy replied simply, without sarcasm or anger, "Yes. If Mr. Hoover feels so inclined he might call the Medgar Evers home and express his sympathies . . ."

A voice came over the phone, that of Charles Evers. Bobby stiffened, fighting the lump in his throat.

"Hello, Charles," he said. "My God, I'm sorry . . ."

CHAPTER 17

President Kennedy and Martin Luther King emerged from the Oval Office onto the portico, smiling for the cameras. When the press corps had gone, the two men were left alone. They were no longer smiling.

"Reverend King," began the president, "the FBI has learned that some of your people are closely associated with the Communist party."

King was quick to reply. "I can assure you," he said in his rich baritone, "that even though they have been associated, they no longer are. They have assured me, sir. I take a man at his word. Even so, I don't believe that anyone influences me once I make up my mind."

"I appreciate that," said JFK. "But these two men, O'Dell and Levison, are known as Communists."

"Let Mr. Hoover show me proof. He has a long history of attempting to smear good people with baseless charges."

"But, Reverend King, I must be practical. And so, I think, must you. I urge you to separate yourself from them. Senator Eastland and his Dixiecrats are trying to kill the bill by calling the civil rights movement Communist-inspired. If J. Edgar Hoover leaked this to the media it could torpedo this legislation that we both want so much."

King paused momentarily to collect his thoughts. After a moment he replied, "I cannot deny the political practicality of what you've said."

"Then you must act."

"Yes. I will sever my relationship with them."

Jack Kennedy smiled and clapped a hand on King's shoulder. They headed back to the Oval Office.

"So then he took me out in the Rose Garden to tell me that I should cut myself off from Stanley and Jack."

King, Ralph Abernathy, Andrew Young, and some volunteers were relaxing in a rear office of the SCLC in Atlanta. King was angry, but he was not in a bad mood. "What do you think of that?" he asked.

"I guess he's afraid old J. Edgar Hoover is bugging his office, too," said Young.

King laughed. "Another member of the FBI Golden Record Club."

Ralph Abernathy walked over to a wall and spoke directly into an electrical outlet. "Mr. FBI, you there?" Smiling, he turned to King. "Speak up, Martin! Testing! One, two, three, four . . . There's got to be at least one of these things still working here. Mr. FBI? You make sure you get it all down right!"

Everyone laughed.

J. Edgar Hoover's eyes darted across the pages of the memorandum on his desk. His face tightened, his eyes narrowed, his breath became a hoarse wheeze. Suddenly he lifted his head and addressed William Sullivan, his chief supervisor.

"How dare you write a report like this? What idiocy has affected your brain? And I thought you had a brilliant future here."

Sullivan lowered his eyes.

"What could have led you to conclude that the Communist party has 'failed dismally' in its forty-year attempt to influence the American Negro?"

His hand trembling, Hoover picked up the report and thrust it at Sullivan.

"That's the same thing they said when Castro took over Cuba! That he wasn't a Commie! Imbeciles, all of you! And now you're telling me that King is a saint!"

"Mr. Hoover, sir, I . . ."

"Get out of here! And destroy that report immediately!"

Sullivan left. Five minutes later, when he had regained control of himself, Hoover left. After he had gone, Miss Gandy entered with a large notepad. She quickly sketched the position of everything on Hoover's desk. Then she carefully stacked the various piles of papers, reports, files and correspondence and wrapped them with rubber bands. She put a little slip identifying each pile under each rubber band. Then she locked the stacks in a special cabinet along the wall behind her boss's desk.

The next morning when Miss Gandy returned to Hoover's office, she took the stacks from the special cabinet and put them on his desk according to her diagram. As she was about to leave, Hoover entered through his private door.

"Good morning, Mr. Hoover," she said with a smile.

"You're late getting set up," he snapped. He handed her some papers. "Here, file these."

Hoover sat behind his desk and examined everything.

"Mr. Sullivan is waiting for you, Mr. Hoover," said Helen Gandy.

"Where are my Presidential 105 files? They were right here last night!"

"I've put everything back exactly as you left it, Mr. Hoover."

Hoover was getting hot. "Are you telling me I don't remember what I'm doing, Miss Gandy?"

"No, sir."

"Find that report!"

"Yes, sir," she said, picking up a file from his desk. "Here it is. Mr. Sullivan's revised report."

When his secretary had gone, Hoover read slowly through the report. When he finished he switched on his intercom and asked to see Sullivan at once. Sullivan entered and, showing no expression, stood at attention before Hoover's desk. Hoover read Sullivan's concluding paragraph aloud.

". . . We must mark Martin Luther King as the most dangerous Negro in this country from the standpoint of communism and national security."

Hoover beamed. "Good, good! I'm glad you've finally come to your senses, Sullivan."

William Sullivan relaxed. "If I may, Director," he began, "I have an idea which I thought you might favor."

"Let's hear it!"

"Well, sir, once we've exposed King as a fraud and a scoundrel, I think the FBI should identify the kind of leader the Negroes should have, someone who could take control of the leadership after King is discredited."

"Who?"

"I'm working on a list now, if the director thinks it an appropriate idea."

"I think it's an excellent idea."

"Thank you, sir."

A shadow crossed Hoover's face. "You know that Clyde Tolson is in the hospital, don't you?"

"Yes, sir. I hope he recovers quickly. We all do, of course."

"Of course," said Hoover. Then he raised an eyebrow.

"Sullivan, are you after Clyde's job?"

Embarrassed, Sullivan gulped. "Me? Oh, no, sir. Please excuse me."

When Sullivan had gone, Hoover burst out laughing.

That afternoon the director stood in Clyde Tolson's hospital room, holding a large cellophane-wrapped wicker basket filled with fresh and glazed fruit. Tolson, propped up in bed, looked pale and wan.

"Junior," said Hoover softly, "I brought you some goodies. The racing form is wrapped up inside."

Tolson, too weak to reply, acknowledged Hoover with smiling eyes. Hoover tried hard to cover his concern. He set down the basket and tenderly put his hand on Tolson's arm.

"I'm only going to give you so much time to loll around in bed, Clyde. I need you. Things just don't run the same without you."

Tolson blinked, tried to nod.

"We've still got a lot of horses to play, Junior. I won't let you down."

They stared hard at each other, and their looks said it all.

Bobby Kennedy and Courtney Evans had a meeting that same day. John Doar and Nicholas Katzenbach were huddled in the rear of Kennedy's Justice Department office, out of earshot. Even so, Evans kept his voice low.

"The director has urged me to respectfully request, again, that you authorize us to tap Reverend King's home."

"Absolutely not," said Bobby.

"I told the director of your reluctance, sir."

"It isn't 'reluctance,' Courtney. It is a firm and unwavering conviction. We will *not* tap King's home office. Is that clear?"

"Absolutely, Bob."

"Anything else?"

"We've had some disturbing information about the March on Washington; I'll have a memo on it later today."

Evans left. Bobby called his secretary in.

"Angie, tell the president I'd like to see him as soon as possible."

To Nicholas Katzenbach he said, "Nick, how are we doing on our lobbying for the civil rights bill?"

Katzenbach walked over to Kennedy's desk. "About forty more to go, Bobby. Next up is Garfield of Indiana."

RFK hit the intercom. "Angie? Get me Congressman Garfield . . ."

Clyde Tolson, fully recovered from heart surgery, leaned back in the plush seat of the limousine. Beside him sat his boss, reading the *Washington Post*. Hoover turned to his aide, his voice once again businesslike.

"I want you to leak to our newspaper and magazine friends the information about King's connection with members of the Communist party."

"But, sir," replied Tolson, "we received a memo from the attorney general's office just this afternoon stating that King has agreed to sever his relationship with both O'Dell and Levison."

Hoover squinted. "You think I just sleep through the afternoon, or what? I read the memo."

"And you still want to have the news media people leak the information?"

"You better see your doctor again, Junior. It's about your hearing. Yes, leak it to the press. King is not to be believed."

"One last item, sir. With the number of gangsters the attorney general has prosecuted and deported, do you think we should assign him a few bodyguards?"

"Not out of *my* budget. Hell no!"

CHAPTER 18

"Is this going to be a long speech?"

Martin Luther King hated what was coming. Beside him in the Checker taxicab sat his old friend Stanley Levison, a sad expression on his face. As they sped through Manhattan the two men said what had to be said.

"Short and sweet," said Levison. He took a breath and began. "Considering the circumstances, Martin, and the pressure that has been put on you, I suggest that the most prudent thing for me to do in the interest of the movement . . . is to officially withdraw."

"This pains me, Stanley."

"The president is right. I bear him no ill will. In his position I'd do the same thing. Martin, it's more important not to risk the passage of the civil rights bill."

"I suppose we have to give them what they want," conceded King. "But we also have to do what we have to do. Officially, as of right now you and O'Dell are out of the SCLC. But we're going to keep in touch. We'll discuss everything just like always, except that we won't do it directly."

"Are you certain you want to do this, Martin?"

"Stan, you and I are old, old friends. I'm very certain."

"Okay. How about we use Clarence Jones as our intermediary?"

"Fine. We'll issue a press release stating that you and O'Dell have left the SCLC to . . ."

"Pursue other interests? I think that's what is normally said."

"Wait a minute, Stan," said King. He smiled. "You're always writing my speeches and telling me what's best to say. We're not going to say that. We're going to say you left . . . so you could start making some real money for a change!"

The decision made, they could laugh about it.

In the White House the president was almost pleading with the attorney general.

"I know I've asked you this before, Bobby, but are you positive there's no way to stop it?"

"Jack, the March on Washington is going to happen regardless of what we do or don't do."

"It could kill our civil rights bill," said JFK.

"They feel it's *their* civil rights bill," said

Bobby. "They feel they've got to make a stand, in force, here in Washington. They want to make a statement."

"Do you think Congress will be just delighted to have a hundred thousand unhappy people milling around the Capitol? Reminding them of their failure to act?"

"Probably not," said Bobby. "And guess what?"

"What."

"What about two hundred thousand unhappy people?"

Clyde Tolson waited patiently while J. Edgar Hoover put a few things in his briefcase. It had been a long day and it was already dark outside the Justice Department building. Hoover, nervous and fatigued, spoke as if he could not catch his breath.

"Communist . . . agitators are behind this march. I just know it, Junior! I smell revolution."

"Sir, we don't have enough troops to control that big a crowd."

"We'll get more. We must. All it takes is one incident. Some ringleader could try to overthrow the whole government!"

"Then again," said Tolson, "it may be one of those occasions when every radical in the country surfaces. If we get enough cameras ready . . ."

Hoover slapped him on the back. "You're

right, Junior," he said. "Who ever said you were losing your marbles?"

"I have a dream," said the Reverend Martin Luther King, speaking to a mass of people gathered on the steps of the Lincoln Memorial during the March on Washington:

> I have a dream that my four little children will one day live in a nation where they will not be judged by the color of their skin, but by the content of their character. I have a dream today!
>
> I have a dream that one day, down in Alabama, with its vicious racists, with its governor having his lips dripping with the words "interposition" and "nullification" . . . one day, right there in Alabama, little black boys and little black girls will be able to join hands with little white boys and white girls as sisters and brothers. I have a dream today!
>
> When we allow freedom to ring, when we let it ring from every village and hamlet, from every state and every city, we will be able to speed up that day when all of God's children will be able to join hands and sing in the words of the old Negro spiritual, "Free at last, free at last; thank God Almighty, we are free at last."

On Friday night, September 15, 1963, Ethel and Bobby Kennedy shared a late-night snack in the study of Hickory Hill, outside Washington. They sat in silence, watching the eleven o'clock news.

... Yesterday, during services, a bomb exploded in the 16th Street Baptist Church in Birmingham, Alabama, killing four young girls and injuring more than twenty other people. This is the fourth unsolved bombing of black homes and churches in the past month in Birmingham and the sixteenth in the past eight years. The church has been used as a rallying point for civil rights demonstrations. There are reports of rioting throughout the city, and the national guard and state troopers have moved in ...

Bobby angrily turned off the TV.

"I cannot understand what is in people's minds that would allow them to do such a thing!"

"Calm yourself, Bobby."

"I can't! Those people are monsters, not human beings! To kill innocent people, four young girls, during church services!"

Ethel shook her head. "It's strange. I never thought things like that happened in this country. Other countries, but not here, not in America."

"All the words, and all the laws and good intentions, they don't mean a damn!" Furious, Bobby stalked about the room. "The state and local police—they let it happen and then they turn their backs on it. And when they find the bastards that did it . . ."

At that moment four-year-old Mary Kelly came into the study in her pajamas. Stopping in mid-speech, Bobby went to the child, picked her up, and hugged her. Ethel watched them. There were tears in her husband's eyes.

She looked away.

CHAPTER 19

"The man is a liar."

J. Edgar Hoover stood before Robert Kennedy's desk holding the FBI's latest report on Martin Luther King. Bobby looked flustered, Hoover triumphant.

"King broke the promise he made to the president and to you," said the director. "He is maintaining his relationship with Levison through the attorney Clarence Jones. It's all documented here."

Hoover shoved the report at Kennedy, who put on his reading glasses and scanned it. Hoover continued:

"The press is beginning to smell blood. Articles have already appeared questioning who is guiding King."

Bobby looked depressed. He remained silent while Hoover went on.

"To protect the president, Mr. Attorney General, you must authorize a wiretap on King's home phone. It will determine once and for all whether or not King is steering a course designed to bring down the government through civil rights violence."

"There's never been any hint of that, Edgar," said Bobby.

Hoover drew himself up to his full height. "When it comes to Cuba and the Russian influence, the attorney general does not hesitate. He sees it as a threat to national security. I would hate to pick up the paper and read that the attorney general was so sympathetic to King that he was unwilling . . ."

"This isn't evidence," interrupted Bobby. "It's guilt by association."

Hoover just stared at him.

"All right, Edgar," said Bobby, defeated. "All right. To prove that it isn't true, once and for all, do it."

Kennedy signed the authorization and handed it to Hoover.

"Just for thirty days, Edgar. Then we'll evaluate the information and I'll decide what further action to take."

"Precisely," said J. Edgar Hoover.

Clyde Tolson entered Hoover's office with an air of urgency.

"We've got a report from the Dallas office of a death threat against the president."

"Another one?" asked Hoover, suppressing a yawn. "File it with the others."

"No word to the Secret Service or the attorney general?" asked Tolson innocently.

Hoover looked disgusted. "You know better than to ask that, Junior."

On the night of November 20, 1963, Jack and Bobby Kennedy, wearing tuxedos, stepped just outside the doors to the Oval Office for a personal chat. Music from a farther room played softly. Jack lit a long cigar and listened to his younger brother.

"I've been giving our balance sheet a hard look, Jack. It seems to me that I've been more of a liability to you than an asset. I mean, you've got to look toward reelection next November."

The president was thoughtful. "You and I will probably be campaigning against Governor Romney," he said.

"Goldwater, if we're lucky. But it will be you, Jack," said Bobby. "Not I. I'm a rock around your neck. I've lost you labor votes because of Hoffa and the Teamsters. I've lost you the South over civil rights. If I give you any more help like that you may be able to carry Massachusetts, period."

"Nonsense."

"I'm serious. I'd like to resign soon."

"You're too hard on yourself, Bobby. If I ever feel you've become a burden you'll be the first to know it."

Jack smiled, put his arm around Bobby's shoulder, and began to lead him back to the party. "Now, Bobby," he said, changing his tone, "after my second term, and after you've served me as secretary of state, don't you think you'd be a natural to run for president?"

"Jack," said Bobby, smiling again, "you're sounding more and more like Dad."

Two days later J. Edgar Hoover and Clyde Tolson were studying the racing form in Hoover's office when the phone rang. Hoover answered. A moment later he hung up and looked at Tolson.

"The president's been shot."

Hoover buzzed his secretary. "Get me the attorney general."

The two men locked their gaze, waiting.

"Hello, Robert? There's been an incident in Dallas . . . the president's been shot. Yes. Yes, I'll call you back when I find out more."

Hoover placed the telephone carefully on the receiver.

"Tell Shanklin to put additional agents on to assist with the investigation."

"Yes, sir."

Hoover smiled, wet his lips. "And put that damn phone back on Miss Gandy's desk where it belongs."

"Yessir," said Tolson. "Now we won't have to deal with that sonofabitch anymore."

The following morning at 9:30 a distraught-looking Bobby Kennedy entered the Oval Office and looked around. All of his brother's personal belongings were boxed and stacked against the wall. A few workmen were still packing things, but when they saw the attorney general they stopped and left quickly.

For a few minutes Bobby walked around the office, dazed, on the verge of tears. Suddenly he turned. Watching him from the doorway was Lyndon Johnson, the new president of the United States. Bobby hurried to him, his arms spread, blocking the way.

"You can't come in here!" he said, his voice cracking.

Johnson was astonished. "Bobby, what are you saying?"

"Can't you wait? You don't have any business in here!"

"You're making a mistake," said Johnson gently. "I'm president of the United States. You have no business in any way to interfere with my constitutional duties."

But Bobby was beyond reason. "You should not be here!" he said, raising his voice. "You don't deserve to be here!"

Johnson hesitated for a moment, then turned and left.

Behind him the Oval Office door slammed shut.

* * *

"Mr. Hoover," said Clyde Tolson, "this is a golden opportunity for you to be a national hero!"

Hoover, Tolson, Sullivan, and Carthen "Deke" DeLoach were huddled in Hoover's office discussing the aftermath of the assassination. Tolson had the floor.

"Think of it, sir. Lee Harvey Oswald turns out to have in his wallet a library card belonging to David Ferrie. Ferrie, as you know, has been linked with the Mafia boss Carlos Marcello. Jack Ruby, as you know, was an informer for Marcello and everyone else . . ."

Hoover interrupted angrily, "Why do you keep on saying 'as you know,' and explaining to me that Marcello is a Mafia chief? You think I'm going senile?"

"I'm sorry, boss," said Tolson. "I just got overinvolved with details."

"All right, go on."

"Sir, both Oswald and his uncle had direct or indirect dealings with the Marcello family. And so did Jack Ruby . . ."

"What's your point?"

"It's all there, sir! It all fits! The Mafia's involvement with the president's assassination! And it's all yours to reveal to the country. Sir."

Hoover shook his head sadly. "You're the one who's going senile, Clyde, not me."

"Sir?"

"Do you really want me to announce that Oswald threatened the FBI office two weeks ago . . . and we did nothing? That we had wiretaps of two gangsters talking about killing Kennedy six months ago? After forty years Allen Dulles lost his job over the Bay of Pigs! Do you want that to happen to me?"

"But, boss . . ."

"You'd better get some rest, Junior. Take some time off. Clear your head."

Tolson nodded and left. Hoover turned to William Sullivan.

"Bill, tell the Dallas office I want every piece of paper with Oswald's and Ruby's name on it hand-delivered to me, personally, tomorrow."

"Yessir."

"Then I want everyone in the Dallas office disciplined for their negligence."

"Yessir."

DeLoach spoke up. "Mr. Hoover, wouldn't that call attention to our . . . problem?"

"They neglected to perform their duty. They must be punished," said Hoover.

"I agree with Mr. Hoover completely," Sullivan chimed in.

"But if they become disgruntled," cautioned DeLoach, "if someone complained and the media got word of it . . ."

"Mr. Hoover cannot allow such acts of culpable negligence to go unpunished!" said Sullivan.

But DeLoach was not to be deterred. Addressing Sullivan he said, "It could boomerang right back at the director, don't you see?"

Hoover looked from DeLoach to Sullivan, visibly pleased that they were arguing over his welfare.

"Gentlemen," he said at last, "my decision is that they shall be punished. From now on, Bill, we will bypass Courtney Evans. He's finished as our liaison."

"Fire him?"

"Let him wither on the vine. Maybe he'll quit," said Hoover.

"Yessir."

"Too bad about Evans," said Hoover with a wry smile. "The Kennedys were going to appoint him to replace me next year."

He turned to DeLoach.

"Next to me you are the closest man to Lyndon. Starting today you will function as liaison with the Oval Office and the attorney general."

"Thank you, Mr. Hoover."

"That's all for now, men."

Sullivan and DeLoach turned on their heels and walked out. Hoover sat staring into space for a moment. Slowly his eyes closed. It was nap time.

CHAPTER 20

Nicholas Katzenbach waited a few days, then went to visit Bobby Kennedy at Hickory Hill. The attorney general was alone in the library, wearing a black bathrobe.

"Thanks for coming by, Nick," he said listlessly. "How do I look?"

"Well, you look like hell, Bobby."

"I can't sleep," Bobby said, staring into the distance.

"You should take some time off. Justice needs you, but we can manage. Is there anything I can do?"

"I don't think I'll be coming in for a while. Could you, uh, wrap up the investigation of the president's . . . assassination as quickly as possible?"

"Of course," said Katzenbach.

"There will be an investigative body to dig into it anyway. The press will keep it alive for a long time. You know, as far as I'm concerned Oswald acted alone. If there was a conspiracy I'd rather not know about it. The guy who killed Oswald, Jack Ruby, said he loved the president."

"Do you want me to keep you informed?"

"No," said Kennedy. "Not really."

"I'm so sorry, Bob . . ."

"My brother barely had a chance to get started. And now there is so much to be done . . . for the Negroes and the unemployed and the school kids and everyone else who is not getting a decent break in our society. But the new fellow doesn't get this. He knows all about politics, but nothing about human beings . . ."

"Outrageous," said J. Edgar Hoover. "He wouldn't let you in your own office?"

"I should have called the Secret Service and had them lock him up," said Lyndon Johnson. "That's what I should have done. But I felt sorry for him. He must have flipped."

"What did you do?"

"I pitched a tent in the Executive Office Building for a few days until he surrendered the Oval Office."

"You should have fired him on the spot," said Hoover. The director called for coffee and cheesecake over the intercom. Johnson looked nervous.

"I'll fire him when the time's right. Now, what about that Lee Harvey Oswald creep? I don't want to go off half-cocked and start making statements that are going to hurt me later. We're on a nuclear alert right now, and so is Russia. Do you realize that, Edgar?"

"You'll have our complete report in two weeks, Lyndon. So far, everything we have points to the fact that Oswald acted alone."

"Thank God," said Johnson. "Otherwise we'd never get out from under it. Look, I've appointed Chief Justice Warren to head up a commission to independently investigate it."

Hoover was apprehensive. He brightened when the coffee and cheesecake arrived.

Three days later Bill Sullivan walked into Hoover's office and placed a copy of *Time* magazine on his desk. Hoover bent over and looked at it. On the cover was a picture of Martin Luther King and over it a banner reading, "Man of the Year." The director sucked in his breath and slammed his fist down on King's face.

"I want this moral degenerate destroyed! Destroyed! Is that clear, Bill?"

"Yes, Director."

Hoover stalked his office, peering out the windows and hurling orders at Sullivan over his shoulder.

"I want a definitive memo written covering King's Communist connections and his perverse, morally disgusting, and depraved sex habits."

"Yessir."

"I want it circulated to the secretary of defense and the attorney general and to all our friends in Congress."

"Right away, sir."

Hoover's glance fell on the magazine cover again.

"How could they have chosen him? It's ludicrous!"

"As I've said and said before, the SCLC is unalterably opposed to the misguided philosophy of communism." Martin Luther King sat in his living room with Ralph Abernathy, facing a southern reporter and a photographer. He spoke calmly, a smile playing at the corners of his mouth.

"But, Reverend King," said the reporter, "how do you explain the newspaper articles that have appeared here in Atlanta and all over the country stating . . ."

"What are the sources of these articles?" interrupted King.

"Well-informed government sources."

"You mean the FBI. Well, sir, I challenge Mr. Hoover to come forward and provide any real evidence he has that there is a Communist influence on the civil rights movement."

"I guess I don't have to warn you; most people don't challenge Mr. Hoover."

King stood and faced the reporter, his hands clasped behind his back. "Sir," he said, "I find it difficult to accept the word of the FBI on Communist infiltration of the civil rights movement when they have been so completely ineffectual in resolving the continued violence and brutality inflicted upon our people. If Mr. Hoover and the FBI would be as diligent in apprehending those responsible for bombing churches and killing little children as they are in seeking out alleged Communist infiltration in the civil rights movement, we would find it easier to believe him."

The reporter had his story and the photographer had his pictures. They shook hands with King and left.

On July 2, 1964, President Lyndon Johnson sat at his desk in the Oval Office with a handful of black pens. Around him stood twenty-five senior government officials, staffers, and civil rights leaders, including Bobby Kennedy, Martin Luther King and Ralph Abernathy. The cameras began to turn as Johnson took a deep breath and began,

"In signing this historic civil rights bill today, I want to pay tribute to President John F. Kennedy, under whose inspiring leadership this bill was drafted and introduced . . ."

The group applauded, gathering around the desk. Johnson distributed the pens to the various dignitaries present, among them a smiling and fawning J. Edgar Hoover. When he had a moment, King took Bobby Kennedy aside.

"This would have been a very proud moment

for your brother," he said sadly. "I speak for a lot of people when I tell you that we hope you're going to stay in public office."

Bobby shook his hand. "Thank you, Reverend King," he said, and walked away. A few moments later he was standing in the Rose Garden alone with his memories, when President Johnson approached him.

"Bob, I saw you standing out here, and I just wanted to tell you that the country owes you a great debt. Today would not have happened without you."

"Thank you, Mr. President."

"Bob, I'd like to chat with you a moment, if I may."

"Go right ahead," said Kennedy. "I've had some of my best talks right here in this garden."

"This town is a hotbed of gossip, Bob," said Johnson. "Some of the stuff you hear . . . For instance, I've been hearing that lots of people think you should run for president."

"No, Lyndon. I'm not interested in that."

Johnson nodded. "Well, I don't mind telling you I'm relieved to hear that."

"I thought I could have some value for you as your vice president. I've spent a lot of time in the Oval Office . . ."

Johnson feigned suprise. "Bob, I wish you'd spoken up earlier. I had no idea. I went and made a decision. The news release should have been out by now."

"What decision?"

"I'm not going to pick anybody who is in the cabinet or meets regularly with the cabinet."

"I see."

"Damn. If I'd only known . . ."

Kennedy looked at his feet. "I'll be submitting my resignation shortly," he said.

"You sure you want to do that?"

"Positive. I strongly recommend that you consider Katzenbach to replace me."

"Yes," said Johnson, "he's a good man. Hey, I've got an idea, Bob. How about you being my campaign manager? If I got nominated, of course."

Kennedy smiled. "Why, you're a shoo-in, Mr. President," he said. "You don't need my help."

"I have given it long and serious thought. I believe I could make a strong and important contribution to problems that plague New York . . ."

It was Robert F. Kennedy in a radio interview, and driving along in a government limousine, J. Edgar Hoover and Clyde Tolson were listening.

". . . lack of adequate housing, care of the poor, and the rebuilding of the ghettos. Therefore I have declared myself a candidate for the senatorial race in New York."

"Ha!" said Hoover.

"Mr. Kennedy," inquired the reporter, "is this just a stepping-stone to the presidency?"

"There's an obvious question!" snapped Hoover. He turned off the radio.

"Junior, make sure my files on that punk are up to date. Now that he's a candidate for public office, we have a responsibility."

Lyndon Johnson looked at the front page of the *New York Times* and put it down. Sitting across from him in the Oval Office desk were J. Edgar Hoover and his assistant, the new FBI liaison with the White House, Deke DeLoach. Bobby Kennedy was making news again, and Johnson was not happy.

"It's war is what it is," he said to Hoover, "and you've got to protect me. Bobby Kennedy is very popular and he knows it."

He held up the paper. "Look at this. Bobby Kennedy is the choice for vice-president of 47 percent of the Democrats queried by the Gallup poll."

Johnson was disgusted. "I don't want him for a running mate, Edgar. But more important is the scuttlebutt I've been hearing about him and his kid brother, Teddy, plotting to grab the presidential nomination away from me!"

"I've heard that, too," said Hoover. "I still think you should have fired him."

"I don't need you to tell me how to handle him, Edgar," said Johnson impatiently. He looked from Hoover to DeLoach. "What I need is for you guys to do what you do best. I want to know every move those two Kennedys make. I want to know who they talk to, who they meet with, where they go, everything. Understand?"

"Yessir, Mr. President," said DeLoach.

"Use whatever you have to, bugs, taps, I don't care. But I don't want to end up with egg on my face come August in Atlantic City. A convention's an emotional place. Funny things can happen. They're planning to show a film on JFK and the delegates are only people. They could get carried away. Even though he's just declared for the Senate there could still be a draft. The Kennedys could steal it right from under my nose."

"Understood, Mr. President," said Hoover.

Abruptly, Johnson looked at DeLoach. "Would you excuse us a moment?"

When DeLoach had gone, Hoover opened his briefcase and handed Johnson a box of recording tapes.

"A compilation of the private life of Martin Luther King, Jr.," he said.

The president did not look pleased. He put the tapes in a drawer and stared at Hoover.

"You been feeling all right, Edgar?"

"Tip-top, sir. Why?"

"You've been acting kind of, I don't know, worn out."

"I have?"

"This DeLoach, now. He's a bright guy, Edgar. He's full of enthusiasm and energy."

"I knew he'd be perfect for you," said Hoover.

"You know what he did? I had a direct line installed in his bedroom right to the White House switchboard so I could reach him at night."

Hoover's eyes tightened, but he said nothing. He knew what was coming.

"You're going to hit the mandatory retirement age in a few months, aren't you, Edgar?" asked the president.

"Yes, sir. Shortly after you have been re-elected. I'll be seventy on January the first."

"You've had quite a career."

"I want to continue." Hoover was almost pleading. "You know that, Mr. President."

"We both want to continue, don't we, Edgar? Nothing's changed."

"No, sir."

Johnson thought for a moment.

"Tell you what. You see to it that the Kennedys don't steal my presidential nomination at the Democratic Convention and I'll figure out a way to let you continue."

"I will protect you, Mr. President."

Johnson laughed. "I hope you didn't say that to the last guy who sat here."

Hoover lowered his eyes.

"One more thing, Edgar," said Johnson, standing. "I want you to find those three civil rights workers who disappeared in Mississippi. I'm getting a lot of heat about that."

"Yes, Mr. President."

The conference was over.

CHAPTER 21

William Sullivan was on the phone when Clyde Tolson breezed into his office at the Justice Department. Tolson lowered his voice.

"There won't be any paperwork on this, Bill, but as of tomorrow we're taking thirty of your men from Domestic Intelligence."

"May I ask what for?"

"Special assignment. Atlantic City."

"Ah," said Sullivan. "The Democratic Convention."

"Right. You are not to discuss this with anyone."

As Tolson left, Sullivan shook his head wearily.

At the podium of the Atlantic City convention, Bobby Kennedy wound up his speech.

. . . I realize as an individual, that we can't just look back. We must look forward. When I think of President Kennedy I think of what Shakespeare wrote in *Romeo and Juliet:*
When he shall die take him and cut him out in little stars.
And he will make the face of Heaven so fine,
That all the world will be in love with night,
And pay no worship to the garish sun.

The delegates reacted, many of them crying, all of them cheering.

On the night of October 14, 1964, Martin Luther King was in an Atlanta hospital bed, recovering from exhaustion, when his wife arrived. In Coretta King's hand was a telegram, but for the moment she said nothing about it.

"How are you feeling, Martin?"

"Same way I was feeling when you asked me this afternoon. Like my circuits are all worn out. What's going on, Coretta?"

She showed him the telegram informing him that he had won the Nobel Peace Prize. There were tears in her eyes.

"You won, Martin! I just couldn't believe it."

King read the telegram twice, then embraced his wife.

"I can't believe it either," he said. "But I'll accept it anyway."

"You also get a big fat check, Martin."

"I was just thinking of that. We'll have to decide how to divide it among SCLC, CORE, SNCC and . . ."

Coretta stopped smiling. "And us. Don't forget us."

"The money's not ours," he said.

"No? The check is going to have your name on it. You're the one getting the award and the money. You deserve some of it."

"Coretta . . ."

"I'm not talking about mink coats and diamond rings, Martin. I'm thinking about our refrigerator that keeps breaking down and . . ."

"But, Coretta, you don't understand. I . . . we get to keep the honor . . . that's for us. But not the money . . ."

Coretta was firm. "We should be comfortable, Martin. The folks who gave you this award don't mean for you to walk around on threadbare rugs and eat out of dishes that are mostly chipped."

"It's out of the question, Coretta."

"We've both made sacrifices, Martin."

"Yes, that's true."

"Well, then. We will both decide what we'll do with our share of the money."

King shook his head.

"No, Coretta," he said. "This is not our money."

They stared at each other in silence.

* * *

Mavis Winters was mopping the fifth-floor corridor of the Justice Department while listening to the election results. When the commentator informed her that Lyndon Johnson won a landslide victory over Barry Goldwater, she shrugged and went on working. But when she heard that Robert F. Kennedy had beaten the Republican incumbent, Senator Keating, and would be the next senator from New York, she put down her mop and looked at her fellow workers, all of them black, and said,

"God bless the man!"

The following day J. Edgar Hoover conducted an informal press conference with twenty-two lady reporters. Deke DeLoach sat beside him, a pencil and notebook close at hand. Hoover was animated, excited, talking too much, and it made DeLoach nervous.

"We take pride in our investigative abilities," Hoover said. "A case in point is the superb work our agents recently did in learning of the location where those poor young civil rights workers were buried."

When one of the reporters changed the subject, DeLoach saw trouble coming. "I'm curious, Mr. Hoover," she said, "to know your reaction to Reverend King winning the Nobel Peace Prize."

Hoover saw red. "King!" he said, spitting out the word, "It was a colossal mistake to give him that award! King is the most notorious liar in America!"

The ladies reacted with total surprise. Hastily DeLoach scribbled a note and slid it over to Hoover.

"Is that for the record, Mr. Hoover?" asked the same lady.

Hoover glanced at DeLoach's note. It read, *"Make that off the record."* The director folded the note carefully and put it in his pocket.

"I would be derelict in my duty if I said anything else," he said pompously. "Yes, it's for the record. Martin Luther King is the most notorious liar in America."

"Mr. Hoover . . ." DeLoach tried to interrupt, but Hoover would not allow it.

"Furthermore," he said, rising from his chair, "in the very near future the public record will show that King's personal behavior is subject to question also . . ."

DeLoach looked on hopelessly.

"What's the matter with you, Edgar? Are you losing your marbles?" Lyndon Johnson, in the Oval Office, leaned forward in his chair and scowled at J. Edgar Hoover. Johnson was furious.

"You and I are friends, or I'd have just put a pink slip in your pay envelope!" said the president. "You can't go around calling people liars! Even if they are! Especially when they've just been given the Nobel Peace Prize, and especially when they are the leader of millions of people in this country!"

"It was ill-timed," said Hoover. "I admit that."

"Ill-timed?" Johnson stood and turned his back on Hoover. "You've got to be kidding! You've embarrassed me!"

"But, Mr. President, I have proof that . . ."

Johnson spun around, looking grave. "I don't care what you've got! I'll tell you what you're going to do, Edgar. You're going to do something you've never done before. Are you listening?"

"Yes, sir."

"You're going to eat crow with Reverend King! You get me? You're going to invite him to come to your office so that you and he can iron out your differences. So when he comes out of your office and talks to the press he'll tell them it was just a misunderstanding and that everything between you two is just peachy keen. Get it, Edgar?"

Hoover was abashed. "I regret that what I said has caused you embarrassment, sir. I will straighten it out."

"*Eat crow* is what I want you to do. And that's all, Edgar."

Hoover began to say something, but thought better of it. He turned and left.

Martin Luther King and Ralph Abernathy were getting bored. As they sat quietly in J. Edgar Hoover's plush office listening to the FBI director's latest monologue, they began to yawn.

". . . Have you any idea how many congressmen and senators, and ex-presidents for that matter, would have given their eyeteeth to have won the Nobel Prize?" Hoover pointed the question at King.

"Well, no, but I . . ."

But Hoover was only pausing for breath. "Every one of them, you can be sure!" he rattled. "Your entire family and your associates, of course, must genuinely respect and admire you for winning that recognition, as does everyone in the government. I've won a few awards in my years of service, but nothing to compare with that . . ."

"We wanted to . . ." interrupted Abernathy, trying to get to the point of the meeting, but Hoover would not have it.

". . . I was just going to relate an experience I had during the war. I trust it won't bore you. There was an acute shortage of housing during the war, and my mother and I had a large but modest home . . ."

King and Abernathy exchanged a bored, frustrated look, but said nothing. It was useless to try.

". . . You can probably understand the crowdedness that existed during the war if I were to say . . . take all the people that attended your March on Washington and try to find basement and attic and garage room for them all . . . By the way, Reverend King, that speech you made was, well, there's nothing else I can call it but thrilling."

"Thank you, Mr. Hoover, but . . ."

". . . Getting back to the housing shortage in Washington during the war . . .

Joseph Kennedy was sitting in a wheelchair on the sun porch of his Palm Beach house. The stroke had cost him his power of speech and the use of the right side of his body. It was night and the furniture-cluttered room, dimly lit by a hurricane lamp, lay mostly in shadows.

Bobby Kennedy entered the room.

"Dad," he began, knowing the old man could hear but not reply, and that possibly he did not understand either, "I had to see you. I have something I have to say to you."

"Nooooo . . ." said his father, the only word left in his vocabulary.

"Dad, I caught myself doing the same thing Jack used to do. I was protecting the family. Jack, you, Teddy—yes, and myself, of course . . . so that the Kennedy name wouldn't be compromised."

"Noooo . . ."

"I told Katzenbach that I felt Oswald and Ruby acted alone. I pray that's the truth, but I'm afraid it may not be."

Bobby moved up behind his father and put his hands on the old man's shoulders.

"With a full investigation we both know what might come out. Judith Campbell. Giancana. The contribution in Illinois. Who knows what else?"

188

Bobby's voice cracked. He came around the wheelchair and faced his father.

"I knew what I was doing, but I went after the mob anyway . . . Have I turned into a coward? Where the hell is my courage? You taught us to put that first all our lives. I'm so ashamed. I'm so confused . . ."

Bobby was weeping. He knelt down beside his father and lay his head in his lap. Joseph lifted a shaking hand and slowly moved it to his son's head.

"I can bury the past, can't I? The past died with Jack. What is important is our mission, our destiny. I'm going to fight. I can still do it! We can still win, we can still go all the way. We'll do it, Dad. We'll do it, I promise!"

"Nooooo . . ."

CHAPTER 22

That same night in Washington, D.C., William Sullivan labored alone at his desk in the Justice Department, writing a letter. At midnight he stopped to drink a cup of coffee and read aloud to the empty room the words he had written.

"King: In view of your low grade I will not dignify your name with either a Reverend or a Dr."

Pleased with his opening line, Sullivan read it again. Then he continued:

"King, like all frauds, your end is approaching. You could have been our greatest leader. But even at an early age you turned out to be not a leader, but a dissolute, abnormal moral imbecile . . ."

Sullivan paused, edited a few words, and went on reading aloud,

"King, there is only one thing left for you to do. You know what that is. You'd better do it before your filthy, abnormal, fraudulent self is bared to the nation."

The FBI supervisor leaned back in his chair and exhaled. It was finally done.

In the morning he showed a small, tightly wrapped package to Clyde Tolson. It was addressed to Martin Luther King at the SCLC office in Atlanta. Sullivan outlined the contents.

"The letter is in there with two tapes of sexual grunts and groans with ladies in motel rooms, and some dirty jokes and bawdy remarks before and after."

"Where's the typewriter you used to write the letter?" Tolson asked.

"It's been destroyed."

"Excellent. Have the package taken to Tampa and dropped into a mailbox there."

Martin Luther King, his wife Coretta, Andrew Young, Ralph Abernathy, and two lawyers sat listening to one of the tapes in the SCLC office in Atlanta. Abernathy held the typed letter that came with the tapes. After a long moment Young turned off the machine.

"Hey, it could have been anybody making those noises," said Young.

"No doubt in my mind who sent you this letter," said Abernathy. "The FBI. We always knew they were bugging our motel rooms and phones. It couldn't be from anyone else."

"They are out to get me, to harass me," said King, distraught. "They mean to break my spirit."

"I'm shocked by the letter," said Young. "Trying to make it appear that a black person wrote it, urging you to commit suicide. It's sick! Isn't there anything we can do to strike back at them?"

"Without proof there is nothing, absolutely nothing we can do . . ."

King could not look at Coretta.

A few days later, Bobby Kennedy stormed into Hoover's office and faced the FBI director across his desk. Hoover was first to speak.

"Yes, Senator Kennedy, what can I do for you?"

"You can stop telling lies to various congressmen and to the press."

"I beg your pardon?" Hoover was irate.

"When I was attorney general I never approved of microphone surveillance—'bugs,' as you call them. They're illegal, Edgar! I only approved wiretaps on telephones."

It was Hoover's turn to fire accusations. "That's the lie you'll have to live with, Senator," he said. "I have affidavits from my agents in the Chicago field office stating that you heard telephone wiretaps and microphone surveillance tapes and uttered not a word of protest."

"Those tapes were never identified to me as

having come from microphones planted in rooms, Edgar."

Hoover relaxed. "Any congressional investigating committee that listened to what you heard in Chicago will be able to tell the difference. And then there was the memo which you may recall, requesting your authorization to lease a special line from the phone company in order to 'monitor microphone surveillance' in New York City. How about that, Bob?"

"I never knew the phone line was to be used for bugging. That was not made clear to me."

Hoover smiled. "What is clear is your signature of approval."

Bobby was furious. "You've framed me, haven't you? You've deliberately entrapped me so that it would appear that I had knowledge of and gave my approval for illegal bugging!"

Hoover rose from his chair. "You chastised me, Senator. You insulted me, you demanded of me that I investigate organized crime. How could I have gotten vital information about those gangsters except by using bugs? You were my superior. You gloried in lording it over me. Don't turn into a whimpering adolescent now that you have to take responsibility for your actions. Face it like a man!"

Suddenly, Bobby leaned across Hoover's desk as if to strike him. He checked himself.

* * *

"I agree that Johnson is out of control on Vietnam," said RFK, "but I don't know how I can believe what you're telling me."

It was late October 1967, and Allard Lowenstein sat talking with Bobby Kennedy in his Senate office in New York City. Lowenstein, thirty-eight, was a veteran of racial struggles in Mississippi and South Africa, and an early opponent of the war in Vietnam.

"Senator," he said, "I've traveled across the country thirty times, all through grass-roots America. I've been listening to the people and I've heard a lot. Believe me, Lyndon Johnson will not win a second term. He's ready to topple and you're the man to push him out of office."

Bobby was hesitant. "I don't want to be known as the man who challenged an incumbent and split the Democratic party," he said.

"Senators McCarthy and McGovern are both interested."

"Oh?"

"Senator, we can win this one without you. Imagine what we could do *with* you."

"I just can't do it," Bobby said, shaking his head. "I want to stop the war, I'd love to dump Johnson, but I just can't say yes."

President Johnson was agitated.

"Mayor Daley's on my side! Truman, God bless him, he's eighty-three, sent word he's one hundred percent behind me."

"Of course," replied J. Edgar Hoover, who

was now seventy-two and moving much more slowly these days.

"The *New York Times* survey said I'll get 65 per cent of the votes at the convention! So I'm sitting pretty, Edgar."

The two old friends sat alone together in the Oval Office, trying to predict and, if possible, to manipulate the near future.

"We've got everything in place as you requested," said Hoover. "We'll know everything Kennedy decides to do the second he's made the decision."

"JFK was popular," Johnson said, "but too many people have come to hate Bobby."

"There could never be too many, as far as I'm concerned."

"So I'm set, right?"

"You have nothing to worry about."

Lyndon Johnson was, in fact, very worried.

"Of course," he said, a gloom stealing over him, "if he beat me in the Wisconsin primary . . ."

"Not a chance," said Hoover.

"No . . . but if he did, I'd be a repudiated president, Edgar. I would be driven from office by the voters of my own party."

"But, Mr. President . . ."

Johnson put his head in his hands and rubbed his temples. Hoover stopped talking and waited.

"I have these dreams, Edgar," said LBJ. "They're nightmares. I dream I'm being pushed over a cliff by rioting Negroes, anti–Vietnam War demonstrators, rioting students, marching welfare mothers, squawking reporters . . ."

Hoover studied his fingernails.

"And then, at the end of the dreams, Robert Kennedy appears, and he's announcing his intention to reclaim the throne in the memory of his brother."

Hoover's eyes focused hard on Johnson.

Hoover regarded the hypodermic that his nurse was putting into his arm.

"With that needle I could win the seventh race at Belmont!" he said with a laugh. The nurse was not amused. She packed her kit and left Hoover's office as Clyde Tolson walked in. Tolson was in poor health from several recent strokes, but ready as always to serve the director.

"Sir," he said, "you were right. Johnson just announced he's not going to run for a second term."

Hoover was speechless.

"But that's not the worst of it. Bobby Kennedy has just declared for the presidency."

The FBI chief regained his wits. "Get me Nixon on the phone!" he ordered.

"Right away," said Tolson.

At dusk on April 4, 1968, Bobby Kennedy stood on a flatbed truck in an Indianapolis parking field under a banner heralding his presidential campaign. A large crowd of blacks and whites applauded until Kennedy held up his hands. His face was quite sad and his heart was pounding.

"I have bad news for you," he said, "bad for all our fellow citizens and people who love justice all over the world . . . and that is that Martin Luther King was shot and killed tonight."

Shocked, the crowd fell silent. A woman began to weep softly as Kennedy continued:

For those of you who are black and are tempted to be filled with hatred and distrust against all white people at the injustice of such an act, I can only say I feel in my own heart the same kind of feeling. I had a member of my own family killed, and he was killed by a white man. We have to make an effort in the United States to understand, to go beyond these rather difficult times.

What we need is not division. What we need is not violence or lawlessness, but love and wisdom and compassion toward one another, and a feeling of justice toward those who still suffer within our country, whether they be white or black.

Let us dedicate ourselves to what the Greeks wrote so many years ago: "To tame the savageness of man and to make gentle the life of this world."

There was no applause, only the same stunned

silence. Bobby lowered his head and made his way off the truck. The sobbing crowd made way for him and quietly began to disperse. In the truck's cab, seated between two black FBI agents, Kennedy broke down and began to cry.

"My God, my God," he sobbed, "what is my country coming to?"

EPILOGUE

Two months and two days later Miss Helen Gandy was watching television in Hoover's outer office. The newscaster's voice was filled with tragedy.

> . . . Most of the Kennedy campaign workers are understandably in shock. The uncontrollable, unpredictable violence that has been raging in this country has silenced a president, the leader of the civil rights movement, and now a senator and presidential candidate, Robert Francis Kennedy. How many more? . . .

"Turn that off," said J. Edgar Hoover, entering his office.

Miss Gandy clicked it off.

The director, followed closely by Tolson, entered his inner office and sat behind his desk. DeLoach was there waiting for him.

"Sir," said the FBI supervisor, "Scotland Yard has found Martin Luther King's killer. He had a phony passport. The Canadian Mounties traced it."

Hoover nodded. "Will the British allow us to extradite him?"

"Yes, sir. When do you want to break the story?"

Hoover thought for a moment. He had an idea. "When is Robert Kennedy's funeral?"

"The day after tomorrow."

"Yes. Well, let's release the story to TV during the funeral."

"They'll have to interrupt their coverage of the funeral for a news story like that," said Tolson.

"Exactly," said the director.

At the end of the day, Hoover and Tolson were on their way to the elevator when Mavis Winters, dressed in street clothes, blocked their way.

"Even though they are dead," said the old black cleaning woman, "they will live on."

"What are you babbling about?" Hoover demanded. "Get out of my way."

"Dr. King and the Kennedys . . ."

Hoover pushed past her, Tolson close behind. Mavis turned and faced them.

"They will never be forgotten. *Never*," she said.

When the elevator doors had closed behind them Hoover sighed. "I don't like it when my enemies start disappearing," he said quietly.

Tolson looked at him curiously, but said nothing.

"I have a philosophy," said Hoover. "You are honored by your friends, and you are distinguished by your enemies."

"Yessir," said Clyde Tolson.

"I have been *very* distinguished . . ."